# Aelred

# of

# Rievaulx

# Aelred

# of

# Rievaulx

Cistercian Monk and Medieval Man

A Twelfth Century Life

**Sharla Race**

Aelred of Rievaulx
Cistercian Monk and Medieval Man
A Twelfth Century Life

First published in 2011 by Tigmor Books.

ISBN: 978-1-907119-02-6

Publisher: Tigmor Books
www.tigmorbooks.co.uk

## Dedication

For Alex, whose patience, love and support
have been truly amazing.

# Contents

# Welcome

In 1110, a son was born to the married priest of Hexham in Northumberland. The child, known as Ethelred, was to become the most influential Cistercian in England—Aelred of Rievaulx.

At the time of Aelred's birth, the land alongside the banks of the river Rye was desolate and wild. In 1134, a newly formed monastic order, known as the Cistercians, acquired the land and began building one of England's most famous abbeys—Rievaulx.

More than eight centuries after its foundation, Rievaulx abbey is still with us. Granted, the abbey is a ruin but it is still able to communicate to us the strength of faith, and the passion and fervour of the twelfth century Cistercians who built it. The location is a beautiful wooded valley along the banks of the river Rye and, even today, it is a peaceful place—the ruins serene, majestic and inspiring.

I first visited Rievaulx in the mid 1990s and have since then seen it in all types of weather and across all seasons. At the time of my first visit, I had never heard of the Cistercians or of Aelred. Something, I'm unable to tell you exactly what, captured by heart and imagination and I yearned to know more.

I soon discovered that virtually all history books dealing with the twelfth century contain some reference to Aelred of Rievaulx. It was even more intriguing to discover that Aelred's own words are still in print and not only are his writings still read, they are discussed and debated by scholars, at times, quite heatedly. Twelfth century Aelred still exerts influence in the twenty-first century, but why?

For historians, through his historical writings, Aelred provides witness to key events of the time including the life and teachings of the Cistercians, the Battle of the Standard, and the consecration of Edward the Confessor. For theologians, his religious writings form part of church history and are as valid today as they were in the 1100s. For visitors to Rievaulx Abbey he is an interesting character who was, and still is, the most famous English Cistercian abbot.

In some elusive way, Aelred's spirit lives on and people, from all walks of life, on discovering him, want to know more. Who was he? Where did he come from? What was his life like? What motivated him? How did he come to have such influence? What was he really like? Aelred captures minds, hearts, and souls and we long to know more about him.

We are fortunate that some of Aelred's writings have survived as well as a biography written shortly after his death by Walter Daniel. Without these, we would be sorely lacking in information but, combined together, they are still not enough. It soon became clear to me that, whilst the basics of Aelred's life are well known—his place of birth, when he entered Rievaulx and the books that he wrote—no overview of his life exists.

Walter Daniel's biography focuses on the spiritual side of Aelred's life and Aelred's own writings are essentially non-biographical. To gain some insight into what Aelred was like and the type of life he lived we have to look further afield and place Aelred in the context of the culture and politics of his time, to look at his family, friends, peers and superiors, and at society in general. Research for this book extended far beyond Aelred himself with the aim of providing a window into a twelfth-century medieval life.

# Structure and Content

The primary intention of this book is to tell Aelred's life story from his birth through to his death. As much as possible I have ordered the information chronologically but there are chapters that are more general in nature simply because we have very little information on exactly what Aelred did in any given year but we do have information on the type and range of activities he would have been involved with.

## Sources

I have relied heavily on Walter Daniel's biography of Aelred as, despite its limitations, it does provide a window into Aelred's life. To attain a greater understanding, and to fill in some of the gaps, I have read extensively about life in the twelfth century and the Cistercian order.

Aelred was quite a prolific writer and careful reading of his historical and religious writings does provide snippets of information about Aelred himself but, as his writings were non-biographical, these are few and far between. His religious writings do, however, tell us a great deal about what he thought and believed.

The interpretation I have given to Aelred's own words is purely my own. I am not a theologian and discussion of the finer points of Aelred's theology is outside of the scope of this book.

## Aelred's Name

Aelred's childhood name of Ethelred, was changed around 1124 when, as a young boy, he left home to embark on a career at the Scottish royal court. Norman ways were sweeping across the country and traditional English names were a hindrance to career development so "Ethelred" became "Aelred".

Over the years, variations on the spelling of "Aelred" have emerged with some writers favouring "Ailred" and others "Ælred". My personal preference is for "Aelred" and it is the version I use throughout this book.

## References

This book is a simple biography about an amazing man. To make it possible to read the book without having to refer to footnotes, I have kept all discussion to the main text. The footnotes only contain information on sources—journals and books—so that you can, if you wish, follow up a particular strand.

Full details of all sources referenced are listed in the bibliography. Aelred's own writings are referenced in the footnotes by his name followed by a key phrase as follows: "Aelred: Mirror of Charity". The full title and the publication details can then be found in "Aelred's Writings" at the start of the bibliography. All the referenced sources are in English.

Sharla Race

# Chapter 1

# Family and Childhood

In England, the year 1110 was one of severe storms, bad harvests and high taxes. May saw an eclipse of the moon, and in June a comet blazed across the sky visible throughout the country for three weeks.[1] It was also the year that Aelred, then known as Ethelred, was born. The country had undergone many changes since the Norman Conquest in 1066 and no one, including Aelred's family, had escaped their impact.

## Ancestors

Hexham, today a small market town in Northumberland, was Aelred's birthplace but his family's roots were more firmly entrenched in Durham. Aelred's great grandfather, Alfred son of Westou, held various positions at Durham cathedral. As sacrist, he was in charge of the room where priests prepared for services and where vestments and other items used in worship where kept. As a teacher, he taught the young boys music and reading

---

[1] Whitelock, 182.

so that they could participate fully in cathedral services. He was also custodian of St Cuthbert's shrine. In the twelfth century, saintly relics were a precious commodity and any church would consider itself very fortunate to have custodianship of them. Cuthbert, with his links to the country's Christian heritage, was well known, highly respected and greatly revered.

Alfred acquired a reputation for a rather obsessive and, from a modern day perspective, unsavoury attachment to the relics of various saints. His actions included opening Cuthbert's coffin to give him a regular haircut, beard trim and nail manicure. There were also rumours that he was instrumental in "acquiring" some of Bede's bones from Jarrow and secreting them in with those of Cuthbert.[2] Aelred, in his treatise on the Hexham saints, describes his grandfather as an influential, wise, respected, and spiritual man.[3]

In about 1020, the bishop of Durham bestowed on Alfred the role of "priest of Hexham" a position that provided him with an additional source of income. Alfred arranged for curates to carry out the necessary duties at Hexham and continued to live in Durham. In around 1040, Alfred died and his son, Eilaf, inherited the role of priest at Hexham—in the eleventh century, it was quite commonplace for priests to be married and for their sons to inherit their positions as priests.

As Eilaf had the far more interesting job of treasurer at Durham Cathedral, he had little interest in Hexham and continued his father's use of curates. It was an arrangement that would not last for much longer and Aelred's family would soon come to be grateful for the living at Hexham.

---

[2] Squire, 5–6, relying on information from Symeon and Reginald.
[3] Aelred: Hexham Saints, 88.

## Norman Influence

After the Norman invasion of 1066, William the Conqueror was crowned King of England and began to radically change every aspect of life within the country. Eadmer, a monk looking back on life from the perspective of the early twelfth century wrote: "We have seen many strange changes in England in our days and developments which were quite unknown in former days".[4]

The Normans brought with them new customs, laws, social systems, military organisations and religious institutions and wasted no time in introducing them. The changes affected everyone. There was a redistribution of the land with control passing to Norman lords; castles, an innovation on British soil, sprang up across the country serving as fortified residences as well as military strongholds. Normans loyal to the new King took over senior church positions and reformation of the English church began immediately.

During the twelfth century, there was a gradual erosion of all things "English". Prior to 1066 there would have been no doubt as to what made an Englishman: his names, speech, customs, law, and even his moustaches and his ale, marked him out as English.[5] As Norman ways spread, it was essential for anyone wishing to get on in society to change: new customs had to be adopted, new forms of taxation and new Lords had to be accommodated, names were changed to their Norman equivalents and even the moustaches were replaced by a clean-shaven look.

The widespread changes did not always take place smoothly. Resistance to the imposition of Norman ways was at its strongest in the North of the country and King William feared the development of an independent territory centred on

---

[4] Quoted in Williams, 1990, xi.
[5] Barrow, 1981, 6.

York. In 1068 an uprising against new tax levies led to the establishment of a castle, sheriff and garrison at York but the rebellion was not quelled. Early the following year, the Norman army at Durham was massacred triggering a similar revolt in York. King William moved north and exacted his revenge.

Fearing the worst, Ethelwine, the bishop of Durham fled from the city with Cuthbert's remains and his clerics including Eilaf, Aelred's grandfather. They made their way to Lindisfarne where they remained until the following year leaving the unoccupied Cathedral to become a shelter for the sick, wounded and dying.[6] Over the next year, the north suffered terribly: thousands of people were killed, and land, property, animals and crops were all destroyed. In the wake of this destruction, food and shelter became impossible to find and thousands more died of starvation. The bishop, clergy and the remains of Cuthbert returned to Durham just before the start of Lent in 1070 but nothing would ever be the same again. Ethelwine knowing he would not be welcome attempted to flee the country, was captured, imprisoned and died.[7]

William the Conqueror ensured that the new bishop of Durham was a Norman who shared his passion for church reform and was, of course, one hundred percent loyal. His choice was Walcher, a nobleman from Lorraine known for his knowledge of sacred and secular literature and, not being a young man, having the experience and wisdom required for the role.[8] He, like other Norman bishops at the time, was shocked at the declining standards in the English church. He was particularly dismayed that the cathedral clergy were predominantly married and was overjoyed to hear that a small

---

[6] Aird 80; Simeon, 687.
[7] Aird, 84–5; Simeon, 690.
[8] Simeon, 690.

group of monks from the south were keen to lead a monastic life in Northern England.

Walcher welcomed the small group of monks, inspired by the great Northern monastic tradition that had thrived under the guidance of monks such as Aidan, Cuthbert and Bede. He helped them settle at Jarrow where they soon received sufficient land donations to enable the establishment of monasteries at Tynemouth and Wearmouth.[9] Walcher hoped that their living example of the monastic ideal would penetrate and influence the secular clergy at Durham and, in anticipation, began building monastic buildings alongside the cathedral. He did not live to see the outcome of his experiment.

As a way of avoiding rebellion, King William had given Walcher the civil and military responsibilities of the earldom as well as the bishopric. It was an action that led to Walcher's demise when, in 1080, he was killed by angry citizens in Gateshead.[10] Once more, the King's revenge was exacted on the North and the result was an even greater level of hardship for a population still recovering from the events of the previous years.

Walcher's successor, William of St Carilef, carried on with the reforming work. In 1083, with the Pope's blessings, he brought monks from Wearmouth and Jarrow to Durham with the express intention of restoring church traditions—an action that marked the start of the cathedral priory of Durham.[11] The existing clergy, including Aelred's grandfather, were given the option of becoming monks and giving up their previous lifestyle, which for many included marriage, or of leaving. Only one stayed.

---

[9] Knowles, 167.
[10] Simeon, 698–9.
[11] Aird, 118; Simeon, 702.

# The Move to Hexham

Eilaf gave up his powerful and influential position as treasurer at Durham and moved to Hexham taking up the position of priest that he had inherited.

Aelred tells us that his grandfather found Hexham deserted and desolate. The church was roofless, trees were taking over the space, and grass clogged the walls. Having made his decision, Eilaf did all he could to establish and maintain a livelihood for his family. It was no easy task and, for almost two years, he was only able to feed his family by "hunting and fowling".[12] The church remained in disrepair and, in his lifetime, Eilaf was only able to afford to build an altar at the East end of the church so that he could carry out his duties as a priest.

On arrival at Hexham, Eilaf immediately began to seek ways to protect his family's future. He was concerned that if the church at Hexham remained under the jurisdiction of Durham he would, at some point, be forced to give up his position as priest. He was obviously still a man of influence as he successfully persuaded the archbishop of York to include Hexham under York's jurisdiction and protection.[13]

Whilst Eilaf struggled in Hexham, the new monastic community in Durham thrived and prospered to the extent that, by 1093, Norman masons and craftsmen had arrived and begun construction work for a new, grand, cathedral. The work was sufficiently completed in 1104 for Cuthbert's translation to a new shrine—on 4 September, Cuthbert's remains were carried around the cathedral in a procession of monks and laid to rest in a stately shrine made of marble and lined with gilt.[14] The new

---

12 Aelred: Hexham Saints, 89.
13 Squire, 8.
14 Sykes, 17.

shrine placed Durham firmly on the pilgrim route and attracted many donations to the Cathedral.

William the Conqueror died in September 1087 and his second son, William, inherited the crown. After more than twenty years of Norman rule, the English had adapted to the changes and William II initially received little challenge but he was unpopular. Whereas his father had vision and plans, William II was more concerned with his own needs and was known for his avarice and double-dealing. His younger brother, Henry, was more popular perhaps because he had been born after the conquest in England and so was an Englishman at least by birth if not by custom. Few tears were shed when William II was killed by an arrow, whether accidentally or intentionally, when hunting in the New Forest and on 5 August 1100, his brother was crowned Henry I, King of England. Henry was to remain on the throne for thirty-five years providing a reasonable degree of stability and peace to a country tired of upheaval.

Aelred's grandfather died in about 1099. His son, also called Eilaf and the man who was to become Aelred's father, inherited the role of priest at Hexham. The family fortunes had improved enough to enable him to clear the encroaching vegetation, repair the church roof, plaster the inner walls and carry out other improvements. His younger brother, Aldred, was in charge of the relics of the Hexham saints so continuing the family's deep passion for saintly relics.

Eilaf can have been under no illusion that he could preserve the status quo and pass on the living at Hexham to one of his sons. At the synod of Melfi in 1093, Pope Urban had introduced the ruling that sons of priests could no longer be admitted to holy orders except as cannons or monks. Papal decrees continued in this vein and, in 1123, Pope Calixtus II, at the First Lateran Council, condemned simony and the marriage of priests. Eilaf would be the last in the line of married priests at Hexham but he managed to escape any great upheaval until after Thomas II came into post as archbishop of York in 1108.

# Childhood Years

Aelred was born at a time of financial stability for his family but one of spiritual and emotional upheaval. An era in the history of the church was reaching an end and, although Eilaf didn't know it, Aelred was to go on to play a significant part in the development of the new era.

When Aelred was still a baby "in his cradle", the family were visited by William son of Thole, a relative who went on to become an archdeacon of York. William saw the baby Aelred's face so full of light that "when he put out his hand, it cast a shadow on the outer side while the outstretched palm, turned towards the infant's face, shone with the radiance of solar light".[15] So taken was he with this light, that he told Aelred's parents about "the incomparable glory which he had seen in their child's face".[16] Aelred's parents were happy that their son had such a fortuitous start in life and declared that "one on whose earliest days such outstanding grace had smiled would in later life be a man of virtue".[17]

This information comes from Walter Daniel and must be viewed as an example of "signs and wonders" that always appear in stories about individuals who grow up to become saintly in some way. I really doubt that Aelred's parents will have given too much credence to their relative's words and the incident was probably quickly forgotten. Walter says that he heard the story from Aelred but given Aelred's humility and

---

[15] Daniel, 71.
[16] Ibid.
[17] Ibid.

insistence on only drawing attention to his apparent faults rather than any positive aspects of his personality, or actions, it seems highly unlikely. It is far more likely that Walter, accompanying Aelred on a journey north, heard the tale from one of Aelred's proud relatives.

Thomas, the archbishop of York, became a frequent visitor to Hexham and was dismayed at the downturn in its fortunes.[18] In 1113, when Aelred was three, Thomas arranged for a group of Augustinian cannons to take over Hexham, restore it and guard the relics of the saints. Eilaf managed to negotiate a settlement that ensured he would retain a life interest as priest as well as various revenues and lands but his power and influence were all effectively removed.[19]

Whilst Hexham was only a small town, it was an important one: strategically, because of its location near the Scotland-England border, and, politically, because of its links with Scotland, Durham and York. It was also a place of religious importance. The church had a respected past having been built by Wilfrid and was the location of a number of saintly relics most notably those of Acca, Eata and Alchmund. Because of these saintly relics, church leaders valued Hexham greatly. York, a key religious centre, had few relics of importance and the York clerics persuaded Archbishop Thomas that he should have the body of one of the saints removed from Hexham to York.[20] The most famous of the saints, Eata, was selected: Eata had been Cuthbert's teacher at Melrose and was known for his role in uniting the church in Northumbria.

In due course, a party accompanied Archbishop Thomas to Hexham to remove the saint's remains but, the night before the planned removal, Thomas had his sleep disturbed by a vision of

---

[18] Raine, lxi.
[19] Ibid, lxii.
[20] Nicholl, 48.

Eata. The saint informed him in no uncertain terms that he would personally be punished if the remains were moved and even struck him twice on the shoulder with his staff. Thomas immediately changed his mind about moving the saint and then fell ill for three days before leaving Hexham empty handed.[21] Given the importance of the relics to Aelred's family, it is quite possible that they had a hand in the creation of the visions and the illness that Thomas experienced. Regardless of the nature of Thomas' experience there was, without a doubt, great celebration in Hexham after his departure.

We know that Aelred had at least two brothers, Samuel and Ethelwold, and a sister. Although we do not know his sister's name, we do know she also adopted a religious life, in her case, as an anchorite. We also know that Aelred had a niece so we can assume that at least one of his brothers was married but there is no information as to their occupations.[22] Sadly, the records available to us provide no information on Aelred's mother.

Our next encounter with Aelred appears when he is four years old. Apparently, one day in February 1113, the young Aelred rushed home and told his family that Archbishop Thomas was dead. His story was not believed and caused much amusement. His family assumed that he had picked up on his father's animosity to the archbishop but, three days later, news reached Hexham that Archbishop Thomas had in fact died whilst on a visit to Beverley.[23] It is difficult to know if the above story is a demonstration of psychic ability or simply an illustration of a child keen to please his father and coincidence.

In 1114, the king appointed Thurstan as York's next archbishop. Thurstan was a loyal Norman and a man of

---

[21] Ibid.
[22] Raine, li.
[23] Daniel, 72.

influence; he had served as chaplain to both King William Rufus and then King Henry I.[24] A few months after his appointment, accompanied by Ranulf Flambard the bishop of Durham, Thurstan visited Hexham.[25] His stay lasted for a few days during which time he will have met Aelred. Whilst neither will have known it at the time, this would be the start of a relationship that would continue until Thurstan's death in 1140.

Like his predecessor, Thurstan was keen to develop York's links with Hexham and became a frequent visitor staying across the village square from the church where the Moot Hall now stands—from the windows, he would have been able to see the children playing.[26] One of his earliest actions was to appoint Asketill of Huntingdon as prior of the Hexham cannons, an action that firmly established Hexham's change from the Benedictine to the Augustinian rule. Aelred describes Asketill as a pleasant man, well able to get on with people from all the different strata of society and a good spiritual director.[27] Asketill continued with the church improvements and arranged for the construction of suitable buildings for the cannons. No doubt, Eilaf played the perfect host and we can only guess at his inner state—resentment and anger at the changes to the traditions that he had been brought up with must surely have been present. No doubt, he made his feelings and views about the latest set of changes known to his family when they were alone.

From an early age, Aelred was surrounded by, and met, a variety of religious men. He will have been told stories of his ancestors, of their journeys and their life in Durham. He will have learnt about Cuthbert, the great age of Bede, and been

---

[24] Nicholl, 8.
[25] Nicholl, 49.
[26] Dutton, 38.
[27] Aelred: Hexham Saints, 92.

familiar with the Benedictine and Augustinian orders. He will have been told about the past and the dreams for the future and I think it is safe to say that he will have been acutely aware of, and thought deeply, about the contrast between his father's life and that of the new cannons. Aelred was, most likely, fascinated by the cannons on his doorstep and probably spent a great deal of time with them regardless of his father's opinion of them.

Aelred's religious contacts were not just archbishops, bishops, monks and cannons. In the year Aelred was born, Godric, then forty-five years old, settled as a hermit at Finchale. Initially he built himself a simple hut about a mile upstream from the ruins we can see today, moving to the site now known as Finchale Priory about five years later. Finchale at that time was an area of woods, wolves and snakes and the perfect setting for one who wanted to escape the rat race of twelfth century living. We know that when Aelred was abbot of Rievaulx he visited Godric whilst on his travels between Rievaulx and Scotland but there are no records of earlier visits. However, as Aelred's family owned land on the opposite bank of the river from Finchale[28] it seems more than likely that they had regular contact with Godric.

I think it will have been impossible for young Aelred not to have been impressed, intrigued and to some extent in awe of the ex traveller, merchant, pilgrim, and, possibly, pirate.[29] Godric's hermit lifestyle also provided a sharp contrast to the lifestyle of Aelred's family as well as to that of the Hexham cannons. Knowing that all three had dedicated their lives to God yet were profoundly different must have been intriguing and, at the same time, confusing.

---

[28] Raine, lxix.
[29] Rice.

Aelred was certainly fortunate as a young child to have contact with so many different types of people and ideas. This early exposure to the religious life in its variety of forms must have laid the foundations for Aelred's later choice of vocation. He would not choose to follow either the Benedictine or Augustinian rule as followed in Durham and Hexham respectively but then Aelred had many more options open to him than his ancestors did. He also had the gift of a childhood during a time of relative political and economic stability—Aelred could afford to be more idealistic than his father or grandfather ever had the chance to be.

## Life in the Twelfth Century

The Norman Conquest had radically altered the land of Aelred's ancestors physically. The cultural and emotional changes were still taking place but, under the rule of Henry I, life for the majority had settled down. As a boy, Aelred did not experience the ravages of war and, like most of us born in peacetime, was not able to comprehend what had driven the previous generation to bloodshed or to appreciate the upheaval and adjustment that follows such conflict. By the time Aelred was a teenager the collective memory of the Norman Conquest was as distant as ours is of the Second World War.

Every day life in the twelfth century was governed by the changing seasons and the vagaries of the weather. Each day started at or before sunrise so that work, especially in the winter months, could be completed by dusk. Things were quieter—imagine life without the ever-present hum of cars, lorries, trains, aircraft, iPods, mobile phones, sirens, games consoles, televisions, generators, air conditioners and machinery that we are so accustomed to. Church bells were probably the loudest artificial sounds that could be heard, their frequency reflecting the importance of religion in everyday life. The population size of England was around two million (in 2010 it was over sixty million) and only about one tenth of the population lived in towns.[30]

Food was not readily available, it had to be grown, harvested or hunted. Salt was essential for preserving food but was expensive. Bread, meat and ale were the main sources of nourishment. Vegetables and fruit were eaten at harvest time, and in season, and were generally seen as the food of peasants. Honey was the main sweetener and not readily available to the majority. Meat, game and fowl were highly prized but fish was almost as equally important as it provided food for the many fast days insisted on by the church. Most of the fish eaten were freshwater fish, such as pike and bream, as transporting fish inland from the coast was not practical.

Travelling was by foot, horse or boat and, given the difficulties this engendered, it is surprising that so many undertook long journeys. Fire was a constant hazard to life and property. The Anglo Saxon chronicle tells us that in 1116 Peterborough suffered a major fire that left the abbey and most of the town in ruins. In 1122 a fire at Gloucester destroyed the monastery and, in 1123, Lincoln was virtually destroyed with many perishing in the blaze.[31] York was also to suffer a number of fires during Aelred's lifetime and it is worth remembering that only the major fires will have been recorded. Life was hard and many, if they survived childhood, died young. Medical care consisted mainly of home produced remedies.

When we look back in history we inevitably focus on the main events and figures but by doing so we distance ourselves from the similarities between then and now. People in the

---

[30] Welch, 120.
[31] Whitelock, 190.

twelfth century were just like us: they wanted work so they could provide food and shelter for their families, they yearned for happiness and sought to find it, and they had to find the internal and external resources to deal with life's problems, illness, old age, death and natural disasters.

## Education

There is very little information about Aelred's education but it is evident from his writings that he was well-read long before becoming a monk. Generally, education was rudimentary often focused on passing on the family trade but youngsters like Aelred, with at least one literate parent, were fortunate and learned to read and write at an early age.

Given the history of teachers in his family, it would be illogical not to assume that Aelred attended some form of school prior to moving to Scotland and Aelred himself starts his book *Spiritual Friendship* with the words "When I was just a lad at school".[32] Schooling was, in fact, more available than many think and, for those with money, was actively sought after in both England and France.[33] Given its size, Hexham is unlikely to have had a school of its own but Durham will definitely have had an education system and schools of some sort. As Aelred's family had strong links to Durham and relatives living there it seems wholly feasible that Aelred was sent to study at Durham and whilst in the city stayed with some of these relatives.

Systems of learning were evolving and establishing curricula. It seems that Walter Daniel's own education was via one of these systems. Comments in Walter's biography of Aelred indicate that Aelred's schooling was less formal than that

---

[32] Aelred: Spiritual Friendship, 45.
[33] Bartlett, 506–16.

undergone by Walter.[34] Walter was obviously proud of his scholastic studies and was even a little snobbish about them. He seems to need to point out that Aelred's writings are more "raw" than they would have been if he had received the same type of education as Walter. As Walter's own writings were never as successful as Aelred's we, perhaps, need to be grateful that Aelred's education was less formal. The subjects that Aelred studied will have included reading, writing, scripture, basic maths and, possibly, some history and philosophy. Durham, after York, was the most important city in the North and will have been the centre of many administrative activities and, I suspect, education.

The main spoken language was still English but French, the language of the Normans, could be heard everywhere and, out of necessity, was being learnt by many. The language primarily used for the written word, whether in books, charters or messages, was Latin. Aelred will have known and used all three languages.

## The Move to Scotland

In April 1124 David was crowned King of Scotland and it was around this time that the fourteen-year old Aelred left his family and joined the Scottish court at Roxburgh. Never again would he live in Hexham or with his family.

Aelred leaving home at fourteen was not an unusual occurrence: once the age of fourteen was reached, boyhood was deemed to have ended and life as a young adult begun.[35] It was, also, a long-standing custom that boys left their families to learn and receive training elsewhere and Royal households had a tradition of training young men, and not simply those of

---

[34] Daniel, 26–27.
[35] Bartlett, 537.

noble birth.[36] For Aelred to have been chosen for a place at the Scottish royal court, there must have been some form of pre-existing relationship between his family and King David.

Because of their location, both Hexham and Durham had to develop and maintain contacts with the key players in both England and Scotland. Hexham had no walls or fortifications—the privilege of sanctuary was the only means of defence it possessed. Roxburgh, which was to become David's capital, when he became King of Scotland, was seen as being "over the hills" from Hexham and at various times during Aelred's life the Scottish border extended as far south as the Tees.

Relationships were based on kinship, trade, and religious ties. As both Hexham and Durham were located on the frontiers of the Scottish kingdom, strong relationships had existed between them and Scotland over the years. For example, King Malcolm of Scotland had always kept peace with Hexham when the Scottish invaded England and he always paid respect to the Hexham saints.[37] Both traditions would be continued by David.

We know that David was a regular visitor to Durham and the surrounding area and in 1117 he is cited as a benefactor of the monks of Durham.[38] In the autumn of 1122, Henry I visited both Durham and Carlisle and it would seem politically astute for David to have been present. Inevitably, there will have been some contact on the Durham visit with Aelred's family. Although Aelred's family were no longer officially part of the Durham church, they were still influential, well connected, and will have been party to major events. Eilaf, Aelred's father, is noted as being a man of influence and he certainly had sufficient

---

[36] Orme: 45, 49.
[37] Dutton, 40.
[38] Nicholl, 45.

personal authority to negotiate the settlement with York that successfully protected his family's livelihood.

As David, the future king of Scotland, was brought up in the household of Henry I he was well known to Archbishop Thurstan. Hexham's prior, Asketill, also provided Aelred's family with yet another link to David: in his role as prior of Huntingdon, Asketill will have had close links with David who was earl of the county. We do not know who was instrumental in arranging Aelred's move to Scotland but the connections were numerous—it could have been his father, possibly Thurstan, another relative, Hexham's Prior Asketill or King David himself.

Some argue that it was most likely as a result of influence being exerted by either Asketill and/or Thurstan.[39] I'm not so sure: Aelred's later writings indicate that he was known to David and that he had known Henry, David's son, from being a child: "I lived with him from the cradle; we grew up together in boyhood; we knew each other in our adolescence".[40] This early relationship is somewhat of a mystery and the records of the time do not seem to contain anything that can help clarify this further. In 1124, Aelred was fourteen but David's son, Henry, was still a child of less than 10 years of age.[41] Is it possible that Durham had what was effectively a boarding school that both Henry and Aelred attended and that Aelred, in some way, was the younger boy's mentor? I think it probably is. David will have wanted to provide his son with an education, and Durham will have been a safe place. If a close bond was formed between Aelred and Henry it would seem logical that Aelred would be invited to join the royal court once David was crowned King.

---

[39] Dutton, 38.
[40] Daniel: Powicke, introduction, xxxv.
[41] Oram, 2008, 74.

The decision, however it came about, provided the young Aelred with opportunities for advancement. Careers in royal households offered good prospects, and promotion was easy for a man of administrative ability; at least one bishop had reached his exalted position from "the king's larder".[42] At the time, men would pay large sums to place their sons in a royal household though there is no indication that this type of agreement was made in respect of Aelred.

---

[42] Poole, 9.

# Chapter 2

# At King David's Court

Whatever route or method brought him to King David's court, Aelred was soon to become an important, valued and respected member of the Royal household: firstly, as friend and companion to David's son, and then in the role of Steward. Further promotion was likely and it is believed that if Aelred had remained with David he would have been given a role such as that of bishop of St Andrews, the most prestigious bishopric in Scotland.[1]

## King David and Roxburgh

David was a powerful figure both in Scotland and in England. Although his loyalties lay in Scotland he was tied to the south through his personal connections to King Henry I. Henry's marriage to David's sister, Matilda, had fostered closer links and peace between the two countries. David, about seventeen at the time of his sister's marriage, became

---

[1] Daniel: Powicke, introduction, xl.

part of the English King's household and received an education and training.

Little is known about David's movements or activities in the early 1100s but we do know that he was left land in Southern Scotland by his brother and that, in 1113, he established a colony of Tironensian monks at Selkirk.[2] In the same year, he married Matilda of Northampton and acquired an earldom. At the same time he became a stepfather to his wife's two sons—Waldef and Simon, Waldef was the youngest.

For David, the Norman way of life was the accepted and expected way of doing things. He embraced the Norman changes, was very much a man of his times, progressive, and keen to develop and further Scotland. He introduced Anglo-Norman procedures, offices and methods; he felt strongly about his native Scotland and strove to bring about change and reform for the betterment of the Scots. To establish his power base he introduced land reforms and distributed land to other Anglo-Normans. He tried to unite the disparate Scottish communities by establishing a national system of justice and administration under his overall control. He encouraged trade and established royal mints and a system of weights and measures. He was also a great patron of religious houses, bringing new orders, like the Tironensians and Cistercians, to Scotland.

David chose to locate Scotland's capital at Roxburgh but during his reign, Edinburgh, the present day capital, also had a thriving royal castle which served as a court residence and the headquarters of the town's sheriff. Roxburgh castle was near to where present day Kelso is but sadly, excepting a few mounds of rubble, nothing remains. David also moved his

---

[2] Oram, 2008, 60.

Tironensian abbey from Selkirk to Kelso and so set about concentrating his power base in southern Scotland. The castle, situated at the strategically important crossing points of the Teviot and Tweed rivers, offered protection to the town and by 1128 Roxburgh was flourishing.[3] King David was a politically astute ruler and was frequently present at the English court: for example, we know that from September 1126 until the summer of 1127 he was in England and working with the English king.[4]

# Life at Court

Adapting to Norman ways would have been easy for Aelred at the royal court. He no longer had to deal with his father's resistance to the changes and, finding himself in a new, exciting and stimulating environment, Aelred could not have failed to thrive. Whether he spoke French or not on arrival is unknown but it is certain that he became fluent in a short time as the business of the court was conducted in the language of the Normans. He was already conversant with Latin and his native English (not the English we now speak). He was brought up with David's son, Henry, and David's stepsons, Simon and Waldef.[5]

The historical records tell us very little about Aelred's time in Scotland but in the first few years he probably spent a great deal of time with David's sons in the pursuit of learning whether it was formally with tutors or informally when out hunting and exploring. We know from his own writings that he developed friendships with Henry and Waldef and that his friendship with Waldef continued until Waldef's death in

---

[3] Moffat: 11, 16.
[4] Oram, 2008, 79.
[5] Daniel: Powicke, introduction, xxxix.

1159. Henry, as the next king of Scotland, was concerned with learning the knightly arts and we know that from an early age Waldef was focused on a religious life. Rather strangely, we know little about Simon at this time; it could be that being a little older, in age, his interests and activities were different and hence his contact with his brother, stepbrother, and Aelred was limited.

The secular opulence of King David's court, the new freedoms and the emergence of adolescence all arrived at the same time for Aelred. Away from his family, he must have felt free, for the first time, to enjoy whatever life offered. He probably, at this point in his life, believed his future would be tied up with the royal household and had no thoughts or aspirations for a religious life. It seems likely that he assisted in certain administrative duties from his arrival but there will also have been a great deal of time available for involvement in the ordinary pursuits of a young man such as riding and hunting, eating, drinking and pursuing women. However, although now in a vastly different environment, he was never far from the influence of religion. Religious services were held regularly within the castle walls and monks, priests, bishops, archbishops, and papal legates came and went.

At around the time Aelred was nearing his twentieth birthday, Waldef left Scotland to join the Augustinian cannons at Nostell Priory in England. Nostell Priory had close links with the Scottish monarchy—they had provided the monks for Scone priory established by King David's brother in 1120, and the prior, Robert of Nostell, became bishop of St Andrews in 1124. Whilst living at Roxburgh, Waldef will have visited the monks at Scone, possibly taking Aelred with him.

Aelred was obviously not inclined to follow immediately in Waldef's footsteps but his friend's vocation must have had a profound affect on the young man. Once again, Aelred was faced with contrasts. As a child he had been confronted with the different lifestyles of his father and the Hexham cannons and now between his own life in a royal household and the one Waldef was to embrace as a cannon.

## Promotion

Daniel tells us that King David was so fond of Aelred that:

> "he made him great in his house and glorious in his palace. He was put in charge of many things and was as a second lord and prince over a host of officials and all the men of the court".[6]

A conscientious young man, Aelred will have taken his duties seriously and it is of little wonder that he quickly became a trusted member of David's household. He probably had various roles around the castle until, at about twenty-one, he was appointed Royal Steward in charge of the administration of the household in particular the food and other essential supplies. In later life, Aelred was to jest that he knew about nothing except catering. This was modesty as the position of Steward was one of great responsibility and trust. Aelred was the first Royal Steward in Scotland and had no idea how important the role was to become in future generations. His successor would be Walter Fitz Alan who came from the Stewart family and the post then became hereditary—Robert, the seventh hereditary steward, was crowned King of Scotland in 1371.[7]

King David, like all twelfth century rulers, was constantly on the move. His travels took him throughout Scotland,

---

[6] Daniel, 3.
[7] Barrow, 13.

England and Normandy but Roxburgh was his main base. Aelred, and the other staff, will have kept Roxburgh castle in a state of readiness for David, and will also have ensured that the King's hospitality was given to all who visited during his absence. Aelred's role as Steward tied him to the area and, whilst he will have attended some events away from Roxburgh, it seems unlikely that he travelled any great distances.

Whilst Aelred was acting as Steward, the country was ravaged by a plague amongst domestic animals, which, like the BSE crisis in the 1990s, must have caused alarm and dismay, threatened livelihoods, and concerned people about the safety of the food they ate.[8] William Malmesbury tells us that no village escaped; that pigs, oxen and hens died, and that meat, cheese and butter became scarce commodities. These types of events must have placed a stress on the young steward not only in obtaining supplies but in ensuring their suitability for his benefactor.

In 1130, David's wife, Matilda, died and was buried at Scone priory.[9] We can only assume that this was a very difficult time for the Scottish court as David was devoted to his wife. He never remarried and there are no records of him having relationships that led to a string of illegitimate offspring as so many of his counterparts did.

## Contacts

Whilst in Scotland, Aelred was, once again, in a position where he came into contact with many of the well known and important people of his time. Even his co-workers were men of influence and well connected: they included

---

[8] Bradbury, quoting Malmesbury, 19.
[9] Oram, 2008, 84.

Gospatric, formerly Earl of Northumberland, in the position of Sheriff of Roxburgh serving as Royal Governor of the castle and as David's representative.[10]

In 1125, a church council was held in the Chapel of St John the Evangelist, located inside the castle walls, and attended by John of Crema, the papal legate at that time. In his role as papal legate, John of Crema became a regular visitor to Roxburgh over the next two years.[11] St John's chapel served as a venue for various meetings including one, in 1126, at which the bishop of St Andrews freed the priory of Coldingham (a cell of Durham) from paying dues to St Andrews. Those present included Bishop Ranulf of Durham, John of Glasgow, Geoffrey of St Albans, and Thurstan Archbishop of York.[12]

Thurstan, already known to Aelred, played a key role in the country's religious and economic affairs and was a great champion for the North. He had travelled with the Pope's entourage, had assisted King Henry in negotiations to secure peace with the French king and had gained a great deal of papal favour. Thurstan was a man of the world—he had travelled throughout Europe, was used to dealing with Popes and Kings, was open to new ideas, was stubborn but righteous, a diplomat and a deeply religious man.

The close relationship between Henry the English king, Scotland's King David, and Thurstan as archbishop of York, was pivotal in the shaping of early twelfth century society. Although they had their differences, each was acutely aware of the need for co-operation to maintain and foster peace and stability. A perfect vehicle for publicly showing their co-operation was in the founding of new religious houses—

---

[10] Moffat, 23.
[11] Moffat, 24.
[12] Nicholl, 103.

around 1116, Nostell Priory was founded by Thurstan, endowed by King Henry I, and had King David as a benefactor. The relationship that had developed between these three men in their younger days persisted and endured, helping to maintain peace and stability across England and Scotland.

When problems arose, as they inevitably did, the Anglo-Norman links between Scotland and England were called upon. Some parts of Scotland rebelled against David and between 1130 and 1134 the fighting was severe enough for David to call upon his Anglo Norman friends for help and these included Walter Espec.[13] It seems likely that Walter Espec stayed on more than one occasion at Roxburgh castle and that Aelred met him. As Walter became the patron and founder of Rievaulx abbey around this time, Aelred will have learnt of the new Cistercian abbey well before his trip to York in 1134.

In 1126, Thurstan consecrated Gilla Alden as bishop of the newly restored see of Whithorn.[14] A new Cathedral was built and Ninian's remains were moved there. King David did not rule the Galloway region of Scotland— it had an independent ruler elected by the area's nobility who, in Aelred's time, was Fergus of Galloway. Fergus was linked with the English monarchy by marriage and with the Scottish monarchy out of necessity. It is possible that Fergus was well versed in Norman ways and it is certainly a matter of record that he cooperated with David, King of Scotland.[15] It was Fergus who re-established the see at Whithorn and, according to Walter Daniel, Aelred knew Fergus well enough to help settle a family dispute in 1159. Given this, I think we

---

[13] Oram, 2008, 85–6.
[14] Brooke, D., 77.
[15] Ibid., 81.

can quite safely assume that Aelred had attended at least one of the ceremonies held at Whithorn whilst living at King David's court.

Aelred will also have been present at the consecration of the church when, in 1128, the Tironensian monastery at Selkirk was relocated to Kelso.[16] The Tironensian abbey at Kelso will have been Aelred's first introduction to the new types of monasticism that were appearing. King David was very much the innovator as the order had only been founded in 1106 and yet by 1113 he had founded a Tironensian abbey in Scotland. The monks wore grey robes and the order was similar to that of the Savignacs. Like the Savignacs, they were overshadowed by the development of the Cistercian order but in Scotland were influential and successful. Other important ceremonies taking place around this time included the consecration of Geoffrey, prior of Christchurch Canterbury, as the first abbot of Dunfermline Abbey; it is possible that Aelred was present.

The early 1100s also saw the development of an order far different from any preceding one: the Order of the Poor Knights of the Temple of Solomon, more commonly referred to as the "Templars". This was a military order formed in Jerusalem after the first crusade to protect pilgrims on their journeys to the holy places. The Templars combination of monastic discipline with a fighting vocation was startlingly new.[17] They adopted vows of poverty, obedience and chastity and, unless they had been out on patrol, they participated in the canonical offices of the liturgy as prescribed by the Augustinian Rule. Their founding member and leader was Hugh de Payens, a nobleman from Champagne. In 1127 Hugh travelled to Europe to seek funds and support for the

---

[16] Oram, 2008, 81–2.
[17] Bulst-Thiele, 58.

new order. In 1128 he visited England and journeyed north to Scotland to meet with King David. Due to the paucity of information on Roxburgh, we have no details regarding this visit but can reasonably assume that he stayed at Roxburgh and that Aelred was introduced to yet another type of religious order.

As the Templars had received twenty-six percent of their administrative sites before 1140,[18] it seems unlikely that King David didn't grant land to the Templars at this time. There appears to be uncertainty of the year but general acceptance that one of the gifts was the manor and chapel of Balantrodoch which became the principle Templar preceptory in Scotland. We know that David's involvement with the Templars continued long after Aelred left his court. In his *Lament for David*, Aelred writes that David kept with him "the excellent brothers of the celebrated Knights of the Temple at Jerusalem, he made them guardians of his way of life by day and by night".[19]

# Inner Conflict

Given the austerity of the 1100s, Aelred had a privileged existence: he had security, the Scottish King's favour, friends and any enjoyments that he wanted. He was in contact with the "celebrities" of the time, had opportunities to learn and study and to be at the forefront of new developments. This son of a married Hexham priest had made good.

Aelred was valued, respected and trusted by those in positions of power, but he was not universally liked. Perhaps inevitably, his position and standing led to jealousy and

---

[18] Gervers, 159.
[19] Aelred: Lament for David, 55.

attempts to discredit him.[20] Walter Daniel would have us believe that Aelred was able to rise above these slurs on his character with great humility but it seems more realistic to believe that he found them irksome and possibly even confusing. The "humility" was more likely diplomacy and Aelred learned well but the seeds of discontent with his lifestyle had been sown. He was discovering the less than straightforward world of politics and was not to know how useful the skills he was learning would be to him in later life.

As Aelred's personality began to mature, his outer world began to conflict harshly with his inner world. Aelred writes of his inner torment, of his disillusion with worldly activities, of his awareness of his mortality and his attempts to find his way back to God. To others he appeared to have everything but for Aelred these things were not enough and he found himself alone and lonely in his inner turmoil. He began to notice the inherent suffering of outward pleasures and enjoyments, realising that all things change and that nothing endures. Life began to feel pointless and empty.[21]

As Thomas Merton notes there was no outward reason why Aelred should be unhappy except that he was one of those fortunate people "who are incapable of deluding themselves that they find happiness in the prosperity and pleasures of the world".[22] Aelred had a calling and he was waking up to it, it was not an easy journey. He knew change was necessary but in what direction, and how, he was uncertain. He became increasingly troubled and confused and, describes, himself as in a state of despair until he began

---

[20] Daniel, 5–9.
[21] Aelred: Mirror of Charity, 133–136.
[22] Merton, II, 39.

to awaken to an understanding that the peace, healing and direction he sought would be in God's love.[23]

I believe that Aelred had a strong motivation to lead a different way of life. He had been dissatisfied with the lifestyle of his father and confused by the conflicting religious directions and attitudes in Hexham and Durham. The royal household provided him with a way out and a new direction but, over time, it became one that did not sit comfortably with Aelred. He was successful and good at his job and no doubt would have received more responsibility and honours but there was an emptiness within.

He had listened to the stories of the great age of Bede and now he was hearing stories of new orders that would return monasticism to the true religious way. The loudest voice amongst these new orders was that of the Cistercians. Aelred will have heard stories about them from various visitors to the court including Archbishop Thurstan. Thurstan had been present when the Pope ratified the Cistercian constitution, in 1119, and had already met, the soon to become famous, Bernard, Abbot of Clairvaux.[24] Thurstan's account will have been the one Aelred most valued as it was based on firsthand experience.

Aelred, perhaps because of the conflicting messages from childhood, never expressed any interest in the existing religious orders. I sense that he was an idealist and that if he was to embrace a vocation it had to be the "right" one. Monasticism in England was undergoing radical changes and development. New orders were appearing and a rather fundamental change in the way new members were recruited into monasteries was gradually establishing itself. Aelred's

---

[23] Aelred: Mirror of Charity, 133–136.
[24] Nicholl, 71.

experience will have been of oblates—children literally given to the monasteries where they were looked after and schooled and most often became monks. This system was soon to fall into decline and the Cistercians had as part of their rule the stricture that only adults could enter the monastery.

If Aelred was already thinking about a religious way of life, but wasn't inspired by the existing orders, then surely the Cistercian ideal must have fired his imagination as it did that of many of the brightest men of his time. We know Aelred had heard many stories about the Cistercians and will have known about their arrival in England. The first English Cistercian house was founded in 1128, just twenty years after the order was formed, at Waverley in Surrey by the bishop of Winchester; it was a daughter house of the French Cistercian abbey at L'Aumône in Normandy which was itself a daughter house of Cîteaux.

The more exciting news must have been when, in 1131, a group of monks from Clairvaux presented themselves at the court of King Henry I. They carried with them a letter from Bernard of Clairvaux outlining the monks' intention to found a Cistercian Abbey on English soil.[25] Walter Espec was a regular at King Henry's court and could very well have been present at this meeting.[26] In 1121 Walter Espec had founded the Augustinian priory at Kirkham.[27] He now extended his patronage to the Cistercians and became the founder of Rievaulx Abbey in North Yorkshire, just a couple of miles away from his castle in Helmsley. He granted the abbey's site in 1131 and the foundation ceremony took place on 5 March 1132.

---

[25] Robinson: Burton, introduction, 14–16.
[26] Jamroziak, 31.
[27] Burton, 79.

Foundation ceremonies were an important event and were attended by many noblemen, local aristocracy, knights, tenants, bishops and other officials. The church, at this point only a temporary structure, will have been consecrated. Very little else will have been present on the site and work on building of temporary lodgings for the monks probably took a further year.[28] The negotiations with Bernard of Clairvaux had heavily involved Thurstan, and King David was certainly sufficiently interested and impressed to offer assistance from the outset.[29] Rievaulx became a daughter house of Clairvaux where Bernard was abbot, and the first abbot of Rievaulx, William, was an Englishman who had been Bernard's secretary. The remainder of the group included Yorkshire men who had travelled to France to join the Cistercians at Clairvaux.

# The Path to Rievaulx

In 1134, David sent Aelred south to see Archbishop Thurstan in York. The mission was probably concerned with the ongoing discussions about whether York had jurisdiction over the Scottish bishops or not.

If David was the astute man he has been made out to be he will have noticed that Aelred was not happy and discussed his future with him. Perhaps the trip south to York was David's way of giving the young man he so valued a respite from the demands of the royal court or an excuse for him to be able to visit the Cistercians at Rievaulx. Either way, it was a decision that was to change Aelred's life.

Whilst in York, Aelred sought and received an introduction from Archbishop Thurstan to Rievaulx. After

---

[28] Ibid., 32.
[29] Knowles, 243.

spending a night at Walter Espec's castle in Helmsley, he planned to visit Rievaulx abbey to see for himself the monks whose reputation for piety, poverty and a return to true monasticism was already spreading and most certainly was a talking point amongst nobles.[30]

The following morning, Aelred was accompanied along the short journey to Rievaulx by Walter Espec and a few others. Externally there was little to see that was attractive. There will simply have been a few wooden buildings in a clearing but everything about the place will surely have exuded silence, simplicity and austerity. They were met by the prior, guest master, and the keeper of the gate. Aelred was allowed to sit in on prayers and was given the opportunity to air his thoughts.[31] He was deeply moved by the men he met and the life they were leading. On rejoining his companions he returned to Helmsley castle for another night.

The next day, as planned, he set out with his servants for Scotland. The route took them along the hill that overlooks the valley in which Rievaulx abbey is situated. Pausing at the top of the road, Aelred asked one of his servants if he would like to go down to the abbey again. The man, who we know nothing about, said yes and the group made their way to the gatehouse.[32] Merton describes the moment beautifully when he writes about the misty valley, the wooden roofs of the abbey, twisting columns of smoke from the bake-house, the sound of the bell summoning monks to prayer, the suns golden rays on the adjoining fields.[33] How could Aelred resist the call of his soul any longer?

---

[30] Daniel, 10-13.
[31] Ibid, 14.
[32] Ibid, 14-15.
[33] Merton, II, 42.

Whilst it is a lovely story the way it is told, I honestly do not think it happened that way at all. I think that Aelred had already decided on a religious life and had discussed this with King David. There were, at that time, no Cistercian abbeys in Scotland and having heard about the Cistercians I am certain that Aelred will have felt attracted to them more so than to any other order. David was a supporter of religious houses and himself very interested in the religious life: in his lifetime he founded houses of various orders including Cluniac, Tironensian, Belvacensian, Arroaisian and Cistercian.[34]

King David's mission for Aelred to York was real enough but it was also the opportunity that Aelred needed to make contact with the new order and see for himself. I suspect that when he left Scotland on that journey it was with King David's blessings to join the community at Rievaulx if he chose to do so after visiting them or to return to his position at the royal court.

It is interesting that he sought an introduction from Thurstan when none was needed—Aelred could quite simply have turned up at the abbey. I suspect that King David had recommended discussing his future with Thurstan and that these two older men, who had played such a key role in Aelred's life up to this point, were protecting him. They wanted to be sure that he made the right choice for himself and were providing him with the support that he needed. Both of them seem almost avuncular in attitude to the young Aelred.

Aelred is then not allowed to just arrive at Rievaulx as a stranger but is taken there and presented to the abbot by Walter Espec, the abbey's patron. The fact that he is allowed

---

[34] Aelred: Lament for David, 49.

to sit in on prayers indicates that this was not a typical first visit. As he was a guest of Walters, he had no choice but to return to Helmsley. Again, I would not be surprised if this had been engineered so that Aelred could not make an impulsive decision to join Rievaulx. He had to, for at least one night, sleep on it. Walter will have been a sympathetic listener but also one who provided an alternative view to a full monastic vocation as he was, himself, attracted to the monastic way of life but had compromised by becoming a patron and benefactor whilst maintaining a political and economic career.

Aelred never returned to his job in Scotland. The servant who had said yes also remained at Rievaulx whilst the rest of the party returned to Scotland. David on hearing of his decision will no doubt have been saddened at losing Aelred from his household but is unlikely to have been surprised. If Aelred had stayed with David, he would have risen to a position of secular importance but the happiness that comes from inner peace would have always eluded him and we, centuries later, would be even poorer spiritually than we already are.

# Chapter 3

# Life as a Cistercian Monk

Aelred spent the required four days in Rievaulx's guesthouse before joining the novices to begin his training. Walter Daniel tells us that Aelred's vocation was very clear, strong and purposeful: "the four days of waiting where he was were like a thousand years, so great was his longing and haste to be taken to the novices' cell".[1]

Aelred must have felt a great sense of relief at having, at last, taken the necessary steps to change his way of life. I wonder if his relief was tinged with apprehension about what he had let himself in for as, whilst the Cistercians were still new to England, they had already acquired a reputation for austerity.

---

[1] Ibid., 16.

During his stay in the guesthouse, a fire broke out and spread quickly, reaching up to the roof timbers. Panic ensued with monks, lay brothers, hired servants and guests all struggling to extinguish the fire. Aelred, in a room towards the other end of the guesthouse, remained calm but on seeing that the fire was not being dealt with, took a tankard of cider and "trusting in the Lord's mercy" hurled it into the fire which was then extinguished instantly.[2] Walter Daniel cites this episode as one of Aelred's miracles and tells us that Lord Gualo who was present was deeply affected by the incident: "to this day he cannot forget the impression made by his astonishment".[3]

# The Cistercian Order

A tidal wave of monastic revival was sweeping across Europe and one of the most successful of the new orders was the order of Aelred's choice—the Cistercians. Aelred could have joined any number of different monastic traditions but he chose the Cistercians probably because he was convinced that he had found the "real thing".[4]

The Cistercian order started when in 1098 Robert, a Cluniac abbot, left his order with a few followers to pursue a way of life more in keeping with the Benedictine Rule than that observed by the Cluniacs. They founded a new monastery at Cîteaux near Dijon in France. They made their habits from undyed wool and had only wooden or iron ornaments in their church; precious metals, paint, coloured glass and sculpture were all forbidden. The regime they followed was strict and austere with their days an organised

---

2 Daniel., 73.
3 Ibid., 73–4.
4 Merton, III, 56.

round of prayer, physical labour and more prayer. Food was kept to a minimum and was strictly vegetarian, at times vegan.

Stephen Harding, an Englishman from Dorset, joined the fledgling order and became one of its founders. In 1108 he was elected as abbot and composed the "Carta Caritatis", the Charter of Charity, which laid down the governing rules for the Cistercian Order and was confirmed by the Pope in 1119. The founders were, as Thomas Merton puts it, "consumed with a passionate desire for truth".[5] They wanted to find the real essence of St Benedict's Rule and live it as it was meant to be lived. They eliminated everything that seemed, to them, to be secondary or non-essential to their primary goal of worshiping God. The austerity measures were not a way of punishing the flesh but a reflection of their belief that poverty and living by the labour of their hands was the correct way for a monk to live when following the Rule of St Benedict.[6]

Other monasteries at this time were also living by the Rule of St Benedict and this breakaway movement was not an indication that there was anything fundamentally wrong with these orders. It was more a case of them having not gone far enough in their interpretation of the Rule and the way it was lived on a daily basis. The founding fathers of the Cistercians wanted to get right back to the basics and remove any impediment, or potential obstacle, to their lives as monks—to their quest for union with God.

The Cistercians renounced anything that could involve the monks in the affairs of the world outside the monastery and the abbeys were located "with an eye to the preservation

---

[5] Merton, I, 214.
[6] Ibid.

of seclusion and strict enclosure".[7] The Cistercians became known as the "White Monks" because the habit they wore was made from undyed wool. To distinguish them, the lay brothers wore a brown habit and both, they and the monks, "were forbidden undershirts or breeches, an unheard of austerity in northern Europe".[8]

Although Stephen Harding remained as abbot until 1133 it was not his name that became synonymous with the new order but that of Bernard. The youngest son of a French nobleman from Burgundy, Bernard, at twenty-two, had become disenchanted with the life mapped out for him and, in 1112, with thirty companions, entered Cîteaux. The order at that time was struggling and this injection of new blood changed their fortunes. In Bernard they had a charismatic young man whose spiritual fervour was obsessive and so heartfelt that, when he preached, mothers hid their sons, and wives their husbands, for fear that they would follow him as so many did. In 1115, Clairvaux abbey was founded with Bernard as abbot and the Cistercian order began to grow in a way none of the original founders could have predicted. Within forty years, there were three hundred and forty three Cistercian abbeys throughout Europe.

The Cistercians epitomised change. For example, they adopted the revolutionary approach of having a total disregard for social distinctions—once accepted into the order the individual's previous rank and status were wholly disregarded. It was a philosophy of equality that was not to be matched for many centuries. Theirs was a "utopian goal"[9]—the monastic community under Cistercian rule would be a society united in its love for God, a love so strong

---

[7] Lawrence, 175.
[8] Coppack, 180.
[9] Leclerq, 13.

that it overrode all the social barriers of society. Powicke notes that the time had not yet come "when men of high origin put on airs, and fatigued their brethren with talk of their exalted relatives; the novice who entered Rievaulx was impressed by the total disregard of social distinctions which prevailed".[10]

In later years, the Cistercians would not be able to maintain their high ideals but during Aelred's time the movement was new, dynamic, exciting and attracted men with a keen motivation to make the Cistercian ideal a reality. Aelred was one of those men. Cistercianism was a call to a total renunciation of the secular world, to follow Christ, and like all new recruits, Aelred will have found himself bathed in feelings of euphoria and exhilaration at being part of a great movement of reform. The Cistercians were the new boys on the block and *the* monastic order to be involved with. Their simplicity and purity attracted men who had not previously thought of becoming monks and even monks from other orders. Bernard commented that the reason for these defections to the Cistercians was that the Cistercians were "the restorers of lost religion".[11]

Walter Daniel provides some useful insights into the Cistercian life in his biography of Aelred. He tells us that the Cistercians observed:

> "at all times a discreet uniformity using only so much and such means of sustaining life as will just maintain the needs of the body and their fervour in the worship of God.

---

[10] Daniel: Powicke, introduction, xiii.
[11] Lawrence, 186.

For them everything is fixed by weight, measure and number. A pound of bread, a pint of drink, two dishes of cabbage and beans...

When they rest on their beds each of them lies alone and girdled, in habit and tunic in winter and summer. They have no personal property; they do not even talk together; no-one takes a step towards anything of its own will. Everything they do is at the motion of the prelate's nod...

Personal standing is merged in the equality of each and all, there is no inequitable mark of exception except the greater sanctity which is able to put one man above others. The only test of worth is the recognition of the best. The humbler a man is the greater he is among them, the more lowly in his own esteem the more pleasing in the opinion and judgement of the rest." [12]

The Cistercians were keen to return to the spirit of St Benedict's Rule but they were also modernisers and a number of significant differences were introduced. The common practice of accepting very young boys was rejected—the youngest age a man could be when he joined the Cistercians was fifteen and, in 1157, this was raised to eighteen.[13] The old Benedictine tradition of regarding each abbey as an independent unit was jettisoned, as was the centralisation adapted by the Cluniacs. Instead, the Cistercians adopted "a system of annual general chapters which was oligarchic in that all members were abbots, but

---

[12] Daniel, 11–12.
[13] Williams, 1998, 55.

democratic in that all were of equal importance".[14] The General Chapter had complete control of the order.

The Cistercians were successful in acquiring papal agreement to some other fundamental changes especially in the way the order related to the secular church: Cistercian abbeys were exempt from visitation and inspection by local bishops and the local bishops were excluded from the process of electing new abbots. The abbeys were also, most of the time, exempt from paying tithes—a tax of sorts that provided income for the maintenance of the secular church and its clergy. As Dickinson comments, the Cistercians were "very much a papal darling".[15] Whilst these changes allowed the Cistercian order greater autonomy they also, at times, placed them in conflict with the secular church.

The Cistercians, during Bernard's time, saw themselves as reformers and this attitude, coupled with the differences outlined above, often led to conflict with members of the existing traditional church structure. The Cistercians not only wanted to change monastic behaviour and rules, they also wanted to influence the secular church. They wanted the system changed so that it was more religious and spiritual and that meant an end to married priests, inherited positions, being able to purchase a church position, and the exclusion of politicians and kings in decision-making.[16] To bring about some of these changes senior Cistercians were encouraged to take up positions in the secular church and, within a few years, there were Cistercian bishops and cardinals, and in 1145 a Cistercian Pope.

It very soon became clear that if the monks were to maintain their required routine of prayer and devotional

---

[14] Dickinson, 105–6.
[15] Ibid., 193.
[16] Daniel: Powicke, introduction, xxxvii.

practices they would need assistance with the daily tasks necessary for bodily survival and sustenance. As a solution, the Cistercians decided to break further with tradition and accept lay brothers, sometimes known as "conversi". These lay brothers took monastic vows but lived separately from the monks. Their primary role was manual work and, unlike the monks, they were mainly, but not always, recruited from the peasantry and were generally illiterate.

## Aelred's Novitiate

Like all new recruits, Aelred had to spend a year as a novice. In the twelfth century, there was no distinct novice's habit— Aelred will have worn secular clothing.[17] One must assume that, in some degree or the other, this was still prescribed but we do not know what it consisted of except for a cloak and mantle.[18]

The purpose of the novitiate was to test the individual's vocation and to introduce him to the Cistercian rule which, for the novices, involved a total change of lifestyle. It was a trial for all and perhaps an even greater trial for those older recruits from established careers or other monastic orders. They had to adapt to austerity, chastity, manual labour, silence, a meagre diet, uniformity and obedience.[19] Aelred gave up everything he owned and the opportunities open to him, to embrace poverty, chastity, hard work, silence, prayer and a discipline that determined how he spent each moment of every day. He was expected to turn himself inside out, to discard all worldly attachments and to totally embrace a religious life. Aelred welcomed the challenge and embraced

---

[17] Merton, III, 60.
[18] Williams, 1998, 56.
[19] Knowles, 634–6.

the peace and freedom from the noise and demands of the secular world. His learning and knowledge of the scriptures begun at this time is clearly demonstrated in his writings.

At twenty-five his personality will have been well formed but no matter how strong Aelred's desire was for his new life he must, at times, have struggled to let go of his old ways. From his home in Hexham to life in a royal household and now to a partially built abbey with none of the basic comforts such as a fire when cold, food when hungry, sleep when you needed it, or comfortable clothes. The abbey was still a series of temporary wooden buildings down by the river. It wasn't until about 1135 that masons began cutting the stone from a local quarry for the church and construction was to continue for many years.

Rievaulx was already popular when Aelred joined and it is likely that a number of other men were novices at the same time as Aelred. We know only a little about two of them: Hugh who went on to become prior of Rievaulx and a young man named Simon who was of noble birth. Simon had run away from home and endured many hardships to become a monk at Rievaulx. He seems from Aelred's descriptions to have been one of those people who have no difficulty with monastic life—they are intrinsically humble, quiet, self-disciplined, never losing their patience or becoming excited over anything.[20] Despite rarely being able to talk to each other, Aelred, Hugh and Simon became friends.

Walter Daniel tells us that the year of the novitiate was a hard one but that Aelred excelled and overcame all obstacles. His novice master, another Simon, said that Aelred excelled "in humility and glowed in piety" and exceeded all in his development of charity (love).[21] This Simon was probably

---

[20] Merton, III, 60.
[21] Daniel, 17.

one of the original group of twelve monks who came from Clairvaux and we know that he went on to become abbot of Warden Abbey and that he outlived Aelred.[22]

# The Monastic Experience

In 1135, a year after entering Rievaulx, Aelred made his profession and became a Cistercian monk.

> He "confirmed his dedication of himself by his written profession before the altar in the church. in the presence of all, as the blessed Benedict commands. There he is vested in the sacred robe, that is the habit sanctified by the Abbot's blessing, and henceforth is regarded as a member of the monastic body".[23]

His novitiate over, Aelred's life was now wholly dedicated to finding union with God. Whilst the Cistercians were a new order, the techniques employed within it, including the use of St Benedict's Rule, were common to many Christian monasteries. The differences were in interpretation and implementation. To attain the highest knowledge of God, the correct conditions have to be created. Whilst these conditions are internal ones, the role of the monastery has always been to create the external conditions that will enable the inner ones to arise. A monk's life becomes ordered and disciplined and he is freed from decision-making and the distractions of everyday life. Walter Daniel summarises the three main strands of monastic life as being holy contemplation, sincere prayer, and honest toil.[24]

---

[22] Daniel, 16; Powicke, introduction, lvi.
[23] Daniel, 18.
[24] Ibid.

Some of the changes Aelred experienced on entering Rievaulx included.

- Less food and no meat.
- Basic, functional and rough clothing.
- Hard and functional bedding.
- A change in sleeping patterns—not only were the times regulated but sleep was interrupted by calls to prayer.
- Manual labour and no choice about the work he was allocated.
- Silence for virtually the whole day.
- Discipline.
- A daily routine that had to be followed.
- A lack of freedom to make any choices.
- Equality.
- No personal possessions.

Aelred's aim will have been to arrive at a state of "knowing" and to do that he would first have to experience "unknowing" hence the ritual process of leaving everything behind. This type of internal transformation does not rely on book learning or intellectual understanding. However, the transformation process needs to start somewhere and hence the reading, contemplation and recitation of scripture—these acted as a starting place for Aelred as he strove to attain unity with God by feeding his mind with healthy, constructive, thoughts and ideas for contemplation.

## The Rule of St Benedict

Benedict wrote *The Rule* in the early to mid fourth century to enable the formation of monastic communities with a set of rules that would help keep them on course. As union with

God is the primary aim of those living within a monastery, everything that takes place within the monastery must, in some way, facilitate this. The purpose of the Rule is, as Esther de Waal notes, "to apply the fullness of the Gospel teaching to the actual circumstances of daily life".[25]

The Rule serves as a practical guide to help the monk establish and maintain loving relationships with God, others, the material world, and himself. Benedict understood that by providing structure and order in a community it helped create the space and time for God. The Rule was designed to provide for the body, mind and spirit via a daily rhythm of prayer, study and physical work. It is based on the scriptures, was used by Benedict himself, has been used over the centuries and continues to be used today.

It is not a theoretical work but contains very specific instructions. For example, from the section on how the Monks should sleep, it states that:

> the monks "are to sleep each in a single bed... If it is possible, all should sleep in one place, but if their numbers do not permit this, they should take their rest by tens or twenties with the seniors who are entrusted with their care. A candle should burn continuously in this room till morning. They should sleep clothed, girt with girdles or cords... The younger brethren should not have their beds together, but dispersed among the seniors."[26]

And, in respect of personal property, it states that no monk may give or receive anything without the permission of the

---

[25] Benedict, introduction, x.
[26] Ibid., 45.

abbot. A monk may own no items, not even books, writing tablets or pens: "everything should be common to all".[27]

## How Aelred spent his days

Aelred's daily routine was divided into three main activities—liturgical prayer, private reading and manual labour.

Cistercian abbeys were located in areas that would ensure their seclusion from the secular world and the valley in which Rievaulx was founded was no exception. An enormous amount of physical labour was necessary to establish the abbey. Many previous abbeys had relied on income from the ownership of churches, mills, receipts of manorial rents and tithes. The Cistercians shunned these to follow St Benedict's rule more fully. It was their intention to live by the labour of their own hands. The morning hours after chapter were devoted to the physical work of building, maintenance and food production.

The time allocated to manual labour varied in length and time of day to meet the needs of the seasons. In winter, a four-hour period between chapter and dinner was the norm. In the summer there were usually two periods between two and three hours slotted into the daylight hours. Aelred participated fully in the physical work involved in building Rievaulx abbey. Walter Daniel stresses this as he tells us that Aelred was physically weak and experienced discomfort and pain. By giving his life to God, via the Cistercians, he gave away the freedom to do as he wished. Although he would soon achieve more freedom as an abbot, in his early years Aelred had to do what he was told when he was told.

---

[27] Ibid., 60.

The main food staples were bread, vegetables such as beans and peas, salt, abbey grown herbs and spices (excluding pepper and cumin), water and/or beer. The bread was coarse with white bread only allowed for those who were sick and those who had been bled.[28] Milk, eggs and cheese could be eaten but not during Lent, Advent or on September Ember days.[29] Meat, including chicken, pigeon and dove, were only eaten by those who were seriously ill. In winter, the monks had a single meal, in summer they were allowed two meals. The monotony of the diet was at times relieved by "pittances" which were donations to the abbey of food and drink usually for special feast days. It was up to the abbot how often pittances were allowed and a record of these "specials" had to be kept. These treats included fish, better quality bread, cheese, wine and beer.[30]

Outside of what was deemed essential conversation, silence was expected. A room was set aside by the Chapter House known as the locutorium solely for the purpose of speaking.[31] In the locutorium, work details were issued by the prior and concerns could be discussed with the abbot. The reality was that in many parts of the abbey, including the gatehouse and the infirmary, some degree of conversation had to take place but as far as possible silence was expected and if conversation was necessary it had to be relevant and not frivolous. The monks also developed a sign language that allowed some degree of communication.

The chapter house was one of the most important buildings in the abbey. Each day the monks would meet within it. On Sundays and special days a sermon was given

---

[28] Williams, D. H., 246.
[29] Ibid., 245.
[30] Ibid., 246.
[31] Merton, IV, 47–48.

but on a normal day some aspect of the Rule was read aloud and commented on. Abbey business that needed involvement of all the monks was discussed, notices were given, and punishments were meted out. The monks sat on stone benches arranged in tiers and were forbidden to discuss what took place in the chapter with outsiders.[32]

Monks who were ill, frail from age, and weak from bloodletting lived in the infirmary. Monks who became mentally unstable were usually kept in a separate part of the monastery or on a grange. Medical knowledge was rudimentary and relied on herbs to cure many ailments. There was apparently a late twelfth century "Book of Healing" at Rievaulx but no copy has survived.[33]

A regular feature of monastic life was bloodletting which everyone had to endure four times a year. A small number of monks were selected for the procedure each normal day so that disruption to abbey routine was kept to a minimum. Bloodletting was seen as a way of encouraging good physical and mental health but it was a risky procedure that could lead to infection. The amount of blood loss could be up to four pints and inevitably weakened the monks. To help them recover they received extra bread and other food for three days and, during those three days, were allowed to rest and sleep. Those three days of rest, four times a year, "were the nearest to a holiday that a Cistercian monk ever got".[34]

Lighting was subdued and kept to a minimum even during the services that took place in the middle of the night. It was expected that the monks didn't need to read the services or psalms as they had already memorised them. The early statutes provided for five lamps for general purposes

---

[32] Williams, D. H., 241.
[33] Ibid., 252.
[34] Ibid., 253.

including illuminating the steps to the presbytery.[35] During mass a single wax candle stood in an iron candle stand in the sanctuary.[36] There were no decorations within the church. The cross was usually made from the wood and the chalice probably silver. The glass in the windows was plain and there were no pictures or artwork. Nothing was to detract the monks from their prayer and inner contemplation. The monks prayed either standing or kneeling, sitting was generally only allowed for those who were ill.

Like all the monks, Aelred immersed himself in the study of the scriptures. The Cistercians were known for absorbing scripture so intensely that "they actually did their thinking in the very terms of the Prophets and Evangelists".[37] This total absorption of the scriptures is very clear in Aelred's writings which flow as narrative yet are rich with biblical references.

The Cistercian calendar was that of the Catholic Church with a few additions such as feast days for the founding fathers and special commemoration days. For example, the commemoration days included 11 January for dead bishops and abbots of the order, and 17 September was set aside to commemorate the monks, lay brothers and nobles who had died during the previous year.[38] The division of the monastic year into religious "seasons" helped alleviate the monotony of constant repetition.[39] Some of the deviations from the normal routine included:

- During Advent, the book of Isaiah was read in its entirety during vigils and also in the

---

[35] Ibid., 228.
[36] Ibid., 229.
[37] Daniel, 18.
[38] Ibid., 230.
[39] Ibid., 230.

refectory.

- On Christmas Eve night a fire was kept lit in
  the Warming House so that the monks could
  keep warm between vigils and midnight mass.
- On the first Sunday of Lent, scriptures for
  reading were distributed to each monk.
- On Maundy Thursday the abbot washed the feet
  of four monks, four lay brothers, and four
  novices (twelve being the number of disciples).

Although Cistercian abbeys were sited in quiet places away from the mainstream of society they were not isolated or unaffected by the events taking place around them. The guesthouse of all abbeys was in constant use by people travelling and will have been a source of news. Rievaulx's founder and patron was a frequent visitor and being concerned with political events will no doubt have kept them informed. The abbot was also a traveller visiting daughter houses and making an annual trip to Cîteaux the main Cistercian house in France.

# Aelred's Work Activities

Work was an essential part of the monastic day and Aelred

> "approached every action without delay, pride or
> reluctance; he never slackened in his obedience by
> asking the prior to excuse him a task or to let him
> do something else, but strove in the constancy of
> charity to fulfil every order, and with an eagerness
> of spirit greater than his bodily strength he longed
> to do more than he could… Weak though he was in

body, his splendid spirit carried him through the labours of stronger and strenuous men."[40]

We learn from Walter Daniel that Aelred was actively involved in the construction work that will have included cutting stone with a hammer and axe, probably at the Penny Piece quarry that lay just outside Rievaulx's precinct.[41] Given the health problems that Aelred experienced and also his background and education, it seems unlikely that the only work he was involved with was construction. William, as abbot, will have wanted to get the best from each of his monks during this crucial time of expansion.

Aelred could have spent time helping the infirmarer looking after the sick. From the "miracles" that Walter Daniel describes it is clear that Aelred had some degree of medical knowledge as practised at the time—he was certainly able to take a pulse and induce vomiting. Walter says Aelred was "knowledgeable in healing and provident and skilful in preserving health". It is also known that Aelred associated with physicians and that several of Rievaulx's charters were signed by them.[42]

He could have helped with administrative duties, or in the gardens growing herbs and vegetables, or with the copying of manuscripts. Whilst all of these are possible options, it is my view that Aelred had a key role within the abbey that, for whatever reason, has not been recorded. Walter Daniel tells us that William, observing Aelred's

> "labour and solicitude for the good, determined to admit him to the intimacies of his counsel and to the discussion of matters closely affecting the

---

[40] Daniel, 22.
[41] Fergusson & Harrison, 62.
[42] Ibid., 124, n. 17; 247.

household of Rievaulx. He discovered that Aelred was ten times as wise and prudent as he had supposed, and that he revealed and unexpected ease in the solution of hard, difficult and important problems."[43]

It was an era of fast promotions with some monks becoming abbots within three to four years after entering the monastery. It has been commented on that it was surprising that it took eight years for Aelred to have an office bestowed on him—that of novice master.[44] Given Aelred's obvious skills and talents it does seem unlikely that he got away with not having a role other than that of monk for eight years. It also seems unlikely that he would have been chosen as a delegate for a mission to Rome, in 1142, if his only position within Rievaulx had been that of a monk.

I believe that Aelred held the position of secretary to William for most of the years leading up to him being made novice master. In this "personal assistant" role, he will have accompanied William on some of his journeys away from Rievaulx—visiting daughter houses and granges, witnessing charters, meeting with benefactors, and attending the Annual General Chapter at Cîteaux. As William will not always have needed a secretary with him there will have been long spells of time when Aelred was involved in other work and the most likely tasks will have been abbey administration and, when time allowed, helping in the infirmary or the gardens.

---

[43] Daniel, 23.
[44] Burton, 103.

# Rievaulx Expands

During Aelred's early years at Rievaulx, the abbey was constantly under construction as they strove to replace the timber buildings with more permanent structures. Rievaulx was fortunate to have a steady stream of new recruits and benefactors both of whom enabled the work to be undertaken in a relatively short period of time.

Rievaulx was so successful that expansion extended to the development of two new daughter houses within a few years of Aelred joining Rievaulx. For an abbey to take on the development of a new foundation they had to have a minimum of sixty monks at the Mother House.[45] As Rievaulx was able to agree to two new foundations within a year they obviously had many more than sixty. Rievaulx's patron, Walter Espec, founded Warden Abbey in Bedfordshire in 1136 and Aelred's novice master, Simon, left Rievaulx with the group to develop the new abbey. In 1137, King David gave Rievaulx land at Melrose, and on 23 March the abbey church was dedicated, like all Cistercian churches, to the Blessed Virgin. The preparations for this hand over of the site to Rievaulx appear to have begun as early as 1133 when King David granted Durham priory the possession of the parish church at Berwick on Tweed as compensation for the Melrose church which was on land he granted to the new abbey.[46]

Within twelve months, Rievaulx had twenty-six of its monks and probably at least the same number of lay brothers leave the abbey to develop new foundations. It is interesting that Aelred was not chosen as a member of either

---

[45] Williams, D. H., 53.
[46] Fawcett and Oram, 18.

group and I think this further indicates that he was playing a vital role within Rievaulx as secretary to William.

# The Wider World

Outside of Rievaulx, events were taking place that would shape English society for years to come. On 1 December 1135, just over a year after Aelred entered Rievaulx, King Henry I died and the country entered a period of unrest.

## Civil War

Thirty-six years of relative peace and stability gave way to civil war and anarchy. Henry's son, William, had died in 1120 and Henry had persuaded his barons to accept his daughter, Matilda, as heir to the throne. But, regardless of her legitimacy and personal strengths, she was a woman and, having spent a great deal of her life abroad, was an unknown quantity. It was Stephen, Henry's nephew, who with incredible speed had himself crowned King of England and within months his position was strengthened by Pope Innocent II's confirmation of his election. The barons who had previously sworn allegiance to Matilda could now rest easy—the Pope's blessing of Stephen meant that they could no longer be accused of falsehood.

Things however did not proceed smoothly. Matilda was not totally unpopular and her supporters included her uncle, King David of Scotland. Confrontation was inevitable. Plundering raids, besieging of castles, battles, high taxes, burning of towns, looting and starvation all became commonplace as both sides struggled to gain supremacy. It was a futile war and has rightly been referred to as period of anarchy.

David of Scotland's support for Matilda posed a substantial threat to Stephen. In 1137, Thurstan, still in his role as archbishop of York, and as a friend of King David, visited Roxburgh to negotiate a truce. This was a difficult time for Thurstan as he had developed an illness which paralysed his lower limbs and had to be carried everywhere on a litter.[47] Also, his beloved city, York, had been devastated by fire.[48] Neither of these, however, deterred him from making the journey north and he did manage to negotiate a truce. Unfortunately, for England, King Stephen rejected King David's terms and the country was plunged into even deeper unrest.

The invasion of Northumberland began on 10 January 1138 when William fitz Duncan led a Scottish force down the River Tweed, probably from Roxburgh, to besiege Walter Espec's Castle at Wark.[49] During 1138 there were many Scottish incursions into Northern England and, inevitably, there was more destruction and damage. Religious houses, including Hexham and Tynemouth Priories negotiated deals to protect themselves from being plundered. However, it was impossible for King David to honour all of these agreements as he quite simply could not be in all places at all times.

Richard of Hexham recounts details of various encroachments on Hexham Priory's property plus an attack which led to the destruction of the new Cistercian abbey at Newminster. John of Hexham records an incident in which William fitz Duncan had to intervene to stop the Scots from entering Hexham itself.[50] In 1138 the area bounded by Carlisle, Newcastle and Durham was devastated and in

---

47 Nicholl, 218.
48 Ibid., 217.
49 Oram, 2008, 129.
50 Ibid., 131.

danger of lapsing into a condition of complete anarchy. There were many groups of bandits operating who further added to the chaos: one gang is said to have scoured the Tyne valley like a pack of wolves, seizing whatever they could and murdering anybody who stood in their way.[51]

Stephen remained as King and the people, land and animals suffered enormously. The atrocities and battles never directly affected Rievaulx abbey making William a very fortunate abbot as he was never placed in a position of having to choose sides. For the inhabitants of Rievaulx it was clear-cut: the anointed King of England, as sanctioned by the pope, was the true king regardless of any alternative views they may have held. We have no idea how Aelred felt on hearing of the atrocities and devastation taking place in Northumberland as result of the actions of his mentor and patron, King David. We can only speculate that he felt sadness, perhaps some confusion, and concern for the safety and welfare of his family.

In July 1138, Archbishop Thurstan met with the main barons of the North at York. Despite the barons' suspicions of each other, Thurstan was able to unite them in opposition to David. He promised them that priests of his diocese, bearing crosses, would march into battle with them and that he personally would be present. He persuaded them that their cause was a just and holy one. Stephen added force and encouragement to Thurstan's words by despatching a company of knights to the north under the leadership of Bernard de Balliol but this was the only support from the South. The ensuing battle known as the "Battle of the Standard" was a very Yorkshire affair.[52]

---

[51] Nicholl, 228.
[52] Musgrove, 63.

After spending the early part of August equipping and preparing their men, the barons returned to York. They prepared for battle by confession, a three day fast and by the giving of alms. The army then made its way to Thirsk. A last minute attempt at peace was made by Bernard de Balliol and Robert de Brus but failed. Robert de Brus was well known to King David:[53] Aelred in his *Battle of the Standard* describes Robert de Brus as "legally with the king of the English" but that "from his youth he had adhered to the king of the Scots and grown into deep friendship with him".[54] The peace attempt failed. On the morning of 22 August 1138, the two armies faced each other on a moor two miles east of Northallerton.

The English army erected the mast of a ship which they called the "Standard". On top of the pole they hung a silver pyx, containing the host, and several banners including those of St Peter the Apostle, John of Beverley and Wilfrid of Ripon. This was a major event in the area involving all the key players in society including Walter Espec. The battle was fairly short and the English were successful in defeating the Scots.

When this battle took place it was only a few years since Aelred had been a Royal Official at King David's court. Now at Rievaulx, David, his patron and mentor, was at war with Aelred's new neighbours and friends—it cannot have been a comfortable experience. Later in his life, and only after the death of King David, Aelred wrote a treatise on the battle. Aelred's *Battle of the Standard* is more of a commentary on how events lead good men to take part in war rather than an account of the actual events. Aelred's loyalty to King Stephen

---

[53] Moffat, 23.
[54] Aelred: Battle of the Standard, 261.

is clearly evident. He does not, however, lose respect for King David but he does view the Scottish King's actions as sinful and misguided.

## Other Events

The suffering caused by the Civil War was exacerbated in 1137 by a severe drought, the worst in living memory,[55] and on Friday 8 June, York suffered a fire in which much of the city was burned down including the Minster and it even reached outside of the walls to the Benedictine abbey of St Mary's.[56]

On a lighter note, 1138 saw the publication of Geoffrey of Monmouth's *History of the Kings of Britain* which became an immediate success. Intended as serious history it was written at a time when there was a fascination with the past but little information. It is a book that has remained popular and can still be found in our bookshops today perhaps because it is the first time we are introduced to King Arthur in print. Modern historians view the work as mainly fiction but Monmouth insisted at the time that his work was based on an Ancient Breton book. Whatever the intention of the author, or the validity of his writing, the book was embraced by all who could read.

We know that Walter Espec borrowed a copy from Robert of Gloucester and passed it on to various friends.[57] Books were a valued commodity and I am sure that at some point this one did make its way into Rievaulx. We know that Aelred was familiar with the legend of Arthur (it is referred to in passing in the *Mirror of Charity*[58]) but that is not

---

[55] Bradbury, quote from Orderic, 18.
[56] Nicholl, 217.
[57] Daniel: Powicke, introduction,, lxxxviii.
[58] Aelred: Mirror of Charity, 199.

indicative of him having read Geoffrey's book as the story of Arthur had been circulating for many years and will have been recited as entertainment at firesides. Aelred was himself later to write a history of the Kings of England for Henry II, a version that did not include Arthur.

Across the channel, Bernard, now the leading light of the Cistercians, was influencing bishops, popes and kings and writing in praise of the Knights Templar. In 1139, the Pope approved the rule of the Knights Templar giving them privileged status. Despite the romanticism that this new order must have had, men still flocked to join the Cistercians and some of the other orders that were emerging at this time, most notably the Premonstratensians and, the only fully English order, the Gilbertines.

In England, York was a main hub of activity for businesses, politicians, and religious leaders. News from the city will have reached Rievaulx quite speedily with various travellers. One of York's visitors in 1139 was Archbishop Malachy of Ireland. On his journey from Ireland to Rome he spent some time in York where we know he met Waldef who was the prior of Kirkham at that time.[59]

# Family Reunion

The truce that had been negotiated with David after the Battle of the Standard did not include the transfer of Cumbria and Northumberland to Scotland and skirmishes and disagreements continued.

In November 1138, Aelred travelled north with his abbot, William, to arrange the surrender of Walter Espec's castle at Wark on the Tweed. Their mission was successful and the

---

[59] Bernard of Clairvaux, 1920, 66–7.

garrison was permitted to march out of the castle under arms with twenty horses provided for them by King David.[60] This was Aelred's first recorded venture out of Rievaulx. He was an obvious choice for the mission given his close links with both King David and Walter Espec.

Returning south, the group stopped at Durham to witness Aelred's father, Eilaf, being received by the Benedictines into their order. Robert Biseth, Asketill's successor at Hexham, was also present to witness Eilaf transfer the family interest in Hexham to the cannons. We know that Aelred's brothers were also present so there was at least a partial family reunion. It was the last time that Aelred was to see his father as Eilaf died shortly after this visit.

---

[60] Hutchinson, 5.

# Chapter 4

# Promotion and Recognition

The ideal of the quiet life within an abbey's walls protected from the outside world was an ideal that was only realized by monks who managed to avoid promotion. Anyone who had a useful talent, or had powerful connections in the outside world, ran the risk of promotion within the abbey or to be called to a position in the secular church. It was not uncommon for the Cistercian General Chapter to order individuals to accept certain roles.[1] Even Bernard of Clairvaux had to resist and argue his way out of being made an archbishop.

Aelred's abilities and qualities, combined with the strength of his vocation, did not go unnoticed.

## Mission to Rome

Early in 1140, Archbishop Thurstan of York died and it was yet another death which led to disputes and problems. King

---

[1] Merton, III, 62

Stephen appointed his nephew, William Fitz Herbert, as the new archbishop but it had generally been supposed that the role would have gone to Waldef, then the prior of Kirkham. As Waldef was King David's stepson, the new English king probably feared that Waldef's allegiance would be more inclined towards David and hence indirectly to his opponent, Matilda.

It was quite commonplace at this point in the twelfth century for Cistercian abbots, and those of other orders, to take as active a part as they could in influencing the general church structure. The Cistercians, under the influence of Bernard, will have seen it as defending the rights of God and protecting his church.[2] They objected to the election of William Fitz Herbert on the grounds that the most important ecclesiastical office in the north had been tainted by the sin of simony—the buying and selling of ecclesiastical offices.

The most senior abbots and priors in Yorkshire banded together in making an appeal to the Pope; they included William abbot of Rievaulx, Waldef prior of Kirkham, Richard abbot of Fountains, and the prior of Guisborough. The papacy was generally accepted as the supreme appeal court in Christendom and, by 1140, appeals to the papacy had become a normal part of church life.[3]

The first deputation to Rome to present their case to Pope Innocent II, took place in March 1142. It was led by Walter of London, an archdeacon of York, and included thirty-one year old Aelred. Given the importance of the mission, it seems highly unlikely that Aelred had not already been involved in a range of other discussions and meetings

[2] Ibid., 62.
[3] Brooke, C., 80.

outside of Rievaulx providing more evidence that he was already serving as an official of some sort at Rievaulx.

The journey overland and by water will have taken many weeks. During his visit to Rome, it is likely that Aelred stayed at the Cistercian abbey at Tre Fontane which had been founded in 1138. The abbot at the time was Pietro Bernardo Pagnelli who, three years later, would become Pope Eugenius III.[4] It is also likely that, whilst in Italy, Aelred travelled the additional 145 kilometres to Monte Cassino, the birthplace of St Benedict's Rule.[5] On route, and on the return journey, the deputation is likely to have rested at Clairvaux providing Aelred with the opportunity to spend time with Bernard.

Bernard was already regarded as a living saint and cannot have failed to make an impact on Aelred. How Aelred felt about the excesses and obsessive nature of some of Bernard's activities in the name of his faith we do not know. But it does go in Aelred's favour that he never emulated them and although he was also dragged into the political milieu he always seemed to maintain spirituality as his primary vocation. In many ways he was a very grounded individual: although focused on God he maintained a perspective built on common sense and wisdom that enabled him to fulfil his role as abbot so successfully that Rievaulx grew in size beyond all expectation and Aelred became known as Bernard of the North but, that is still to come...

The delegation returned with a letter from the pope summoning their superiors to present their case. It was a dispute that was to continue for a further five years but the first deputation did succeed in delaying the consecration of William Fitz Herbert as archbishop.

---

[4] Fergusson & Harrison, 63.
[5] Ibid.

# Novice Master

On his return from Rome, Aelred was given the important and vital office of Novice Master at Rievaulx, a key role within the abbey only given to men with the right abilities. It seems also to have been a route to promotion. Aelred's own novice master, Simon, went on to become abbot at Warden.[6]

As novice master, Aelred was responsible for supervising the new entrants' year-long novitiate. His role was to guide, advice, and instruct the novices in the Cistercian Rule. It was work that involved counselling and support in assisting men to adjust to a totally new way of life. Walter Daniel tells us that Aelred was very skilful in this role and refused to give up on even seemingly hopeless cases.[7] His desire to see the new recruits successfully through their novitiate was fuelled by his own steadfast vocation. I suspect that Aelred had accepted the way of life so fully that he could not, at that time, envisage any other and will have been filled with a strong evangelical fervour to encourage others to embrace the Cistercian way of life.

His tenacity and patience are demonstrated by the stories of various incidents involving a monk referred to as the "unstable monk".[8] This monk had many doubts and problems and at, various times, attempted to leave his vocation. Aelred was always successful in dissuading him. The importance given to this individual is questionable. Doubting a vocation and having difficulties with the change in lifestyle were not rare events. It seems more likely that the stories are simply used by Walter Daniel to illustrate Aelred's ability in helping men to realize their vocation.

---

[6] Daniel, 16
[7] Ibid., 23–24.
[8] Ibid., 24.

As novice master, Aelred was working with a diverse group of men who all had experience of secular society. They had left their status at the gatehouse but, inevitably, differences will have been visible especially in terms of the type of education, if any, they had received. Some will have been knights and nobles, and others small landowners or clerics.[9] They will all, to some extent, have been both exhilarated and scared. Aelred will have come to know each man well and worked with him according to his level of understanding and ability. He will have been keen to share his own love of the Cistercian life and, having been a monk for a relatively short time, will have been keenly aware of the issues that troubled the new recruits as they made the transition to monastic life.

It was around this time that, at the insistence of Bernard of Clairvaux, Aelred started to work on his most well known book: The *Mirror of Charity*.

# The Mirror of Charity

Aelred was about thirty-two years old when he wrote the *Mirror of Charity*. It was his first major work and, completed, whilst he was Rievaulx's novice master.

When Aelred and Bernard met, in 1142, they will have quite naturally discussed the criticisms that were being levelled at the Cistercians for being too austere. Bernard, impressed by Aelred's arguments and devotion, asked him to write his thoughts down so that they could help others. Aelred, not feeling worthy enough, did not immediately do as instructed.

---

[9] Knowles, 635; Leclerq, 11.

The book starts with a letter from Bernard of Clairvaux: "I asked you, my brother, rather, I ordered you, no, rather I adjured you with God's name as witness, to write a little something for me in reply to the complaints of certain monks who are struggling from more remiss to stricter ways".[10] Bernard gently scolds Aelred for his delay and reluctance, arguing that whilst humility is a great virtue, disobedience is not an act of humility. Later in the letter, Bernard commands Aelred, in the name of Jesus Christ, to write about "the excellence of charity, its fruit and its proper ordering" and to call the finished work the "Mirror of Charity".[11]

The letter serves as an introduction to the book and is a way of ensuring that the readers, primarily other monks, know that the work has been written with permission—a monk needed the endorsement of at least his own abbot to write a book.[12] No doubt Aelred had already received permission from Abbot William but a letter from Bernard "ordering" him to write the *Mirror of Charity* would have increased the book's standing.

The focus of the *Mirror of Charity* is the theological basis of the Cistercian way of life: it explains and justifies the Cistercian way as a sound and true path to attaining union and peace with God. Throughout the book, Aelred backs up his arguments and reasoning with scriptural references to the extent that the majority of the sentences, in some way, link to a passage in the bible. The overall aim of the book is to provide a mirror into which the reader can gaze and compare themselves with the possible, the ideal. It was a book never intended for the layman, the intended audience was always

---

[10] Aelred: Mirror of Charity, 69.
[11] Aelred: Mirror of Charity, 71–72.
[12] Bredero, 36.

fellow monks whether Cistercian or from one of the other orders.

The subject matter is concerned with true "charity" which, in this context, means "universal love". The book is divided into three parts and includes notes and meditations Aelred had already been working on including correspondence to a friend named Hugh who was no longer at Rievaulx but in one of the daughter houses. Book one deals with the nature of charity, book two shows how the Cistercian life helps one attain it, and book three deals with the specifics in detail.

Aelred believes that all men are created in the image of God and are therefore capable of happiness. Within each individual there is a "divine imprint" that, if allowed to come forth, will lead to an understanding of self and God and so provide a true state of happiness. No matter how far removed an individual is from the path by wrong thing, wrong action, and ignorance (what Christians generally refer to as sin), the divine imprint remains within that person.

Aelred outlines Cistercian theology in respect of devotion to God, non-attachment to the material world, chastity and discipline. In answer to critics who complained about the harshness of the Cistercian path, he insists that it could only be seen as such if there was still self-centredness and attachment to the world remaining. Any suffering brought about by the Cistercian way of life was more than compensated for by the tranquillity, peace, and joy that followed in its wake. He further insists that an austere life, the Cistercian way of life, is in keeping with Christ's message and life, and provides the perfect vehicle for finding charity and oneness with God. His argument is developed and presented as a dialogue with a novice he was responsible for.

Aelred moves his argument forward to arrive at a definition of the monastic life—freely giving of self in love.

The book includes a eulogy for his friend, Simon, who had recently died.[13] This is probably the Simon that Aelred met as a novice. From Aelred's descriptions, we can reasonably assume that Simon was around twenty-three when he died and had been ill for around eight years. Aelred paints a picture of a young monk who had reached perfect tranquillity and peace—signs of a pure and detached heart.[14] Aelred uses Simon's life and death to illustrate how the Cistercian life can be fulfilling and rewarding. He further demonstrates this by analysing his own grief to show how important it is to rise above attachment to the material world and to rejoice in God.

The erosion of self-centeredness and the development of love are at the heart of the *Mirror of Charity*. Aelred is very clear that love, in the context of the Cistercian way of life, has nothing to do with intimacy, power, material goods or money. In his pursuit of happiness, man looks outside of himself and develops love and attachment for things and people. He does this without rational thought, feeling driven and compelled to own and possess things and foster relationships. This self-centeredness Aelred defines as a form of "evil" love that always leads to dissatisfaction and unhappiness. "Good" love is the love of God and of others in whom man sees God reflected. Aelred argues that the Cistercian way of life, with all its rules and strictures, provides the individual with a stable environment and foundation for spiritual union with God and that perceived difficulties all help rather than hinder the process.

---

13 Aelred: Mirror of Charity, 147-59
14 Merton, III, 60–1.

Aelred reasons that to love is easy but to love with full self-surrender is much harder. Yet love without service is like the emotion of the theatre-goer who cries at the sight of sufferings which in the street he would pass by unmoved. At this point in the book the novice hangs his head and remembers how he had been so lightly moved to tears by his love for Jesus yet had so easily cried on hearing the story of King Arthur.[15]

Aelred explores the psychology behind resistance to the Cistercian Rule in a way that had not been done before. He is deeply concerned not with laying down the law of the Rule but with showing and explaining how the Rule can help the individual novice find his path to God. He understands the problems and does not minimise them. Rather, he acknowledges them and shows how they can be overcome. Aelred did not settle the "difficulties of the spiritual life by formulas",[16] his method was open and supportive. He operated from such a firm foundation of his own beliefs and study that there was nothing to be threatened within him about his faith, enabling him to listen and help in ways that were appropriate to the individuals under his care.

Aelred's method as such was to enable the novice to find his own way by doing his own reflection and thinking and not just blindly accepting what he was told. Aelred posed questions and suggested trains of thought but did not impose his understanding. He wanted them to have what he had, a deep inner knowing, and they could only achieve that by undertaking their own inner journey. Aelred understood that simple faith was not enough; each individual had to do the inner "work". His acceptance, patience, understanding and

---

[15] Aelred: Mirror of Charity, 199.
[16] Merton, III, 67.

empathy must have made him a much liked and respected novice master.

# Religious Issues

The Cistercians continued to expand and gain influence throughout Europe. New houses were continuously being founded, and there was a steady stream of new recruits joining as monks and as lay brothers. Cistercian influence spread far outside of the order culminating in the election of a Cistercian pope in 1145.

## Dundrennan

Rievaulx's new daughter house, Dundrennan Abbey, about six and a half miles south-east of Kirkcudbright and within two miles of the Solway Firth, was founded around this time. This was not a foundation that was established as quickly or as easily as Rievaulx's other daughter houses and the exact foundation date and details of the early history are lost.[17]

Assumptions have been made that the foundation was instigated by King David but, given the location of the abbey in Galloway, the most likely founder was Lord Fergus of Galloway. Daphne Brooke has traced the foundation to the visit of Archbishop Malachy of Ireland, in 1139, and notes that Dundrennan was a working community by midsummer 1142.[18] It could be the case that Fergus saw the founding of a monastery as a way of making spiritual amends for the atrocities of war in the previous years and for taking up arms against the archbishop of York during the Battle of the Standard.

---

[17] Christie, 11.
[18] Brooke, D., 89.

## Waldef's Defection

The debate about the election of the new archbishop of York continued and Waldef was in the next delegation to visit Rome in 1143. Inevitably, he will have spent time with Bernard at Clairvaux and met many other Cistercians. It was a trip that proved to be a turning point in his life.

A few months after his return Waldef gave up his post as prior of Kirkham and joined the Cistercians. He began his novitiate at Warden abbey in Bedfordshire, Rievaulx's first daughter house. Waldef's rejection of the Augustinian way of life caused a great deal of upset. The cannons were shocked and distressed at the defection of their prior and some wanted to follow him. The Kirkham cannons appealed for help to Simon, the Earl of Northampton and Waldef's brother.

Simon, for whatever reason, viewed Waldef's choice with great disfavour and joined the protest with vigour even going as far as threatening to burn Warden abbey "to the ground unless Waldef was sent away".[19] In the twelfth century, threats such as these could easily turn into reality and so, in order to protect the monks at Warden from Simon's wrath, Waldef was moved to Rievaulx to complete his novitiate. For a period of time the very existence of Kirkham as an Augustinian house was threatened but in the end none of the cannons followed Waldef and the dust began to settle.

Aelred must have been delighted in his friend's choice but Waldef was not to find his initiation into Cistercian life as easy as Aelred says his own was. Waldef's biographer, Jocelin of Furness, tells us that Waldef had periods of great doubt and depression. He found the food coarse and unappetising, the garments rough, the manual labour and

---

[19] Merton, quote from Jocelin of Furness, IV, 54.

endless round of devotional practices tough going. He yearned for a less austere life and had doubts that the Cistercian rule was truly the best path for the salvation of the soul. He persevered and worked through his doubts and overcame the problems of his new way of life, completed his novitiate and remained at Rievaulx as a monk. By 1148 he held the position of sacrist.[20]

## York's Archbishop

The mission to Rome that Waldef and, at an earlier stager Aelred, had been involved with did not succeed in having King Stephen's chosen candidate overturned, and William Fitzherbert was consecrated as York's archbishop. This, however, did not resolve the situation—William had not yet been granted the pallium and, unfortunately for him, Innocent II died later in the year and the following two popes also died in quick succession.

## Cistercian Pope

In 1145 Eugenius III, a Cistercian, was elected as Pope and deposed William as York's archbishop. In 1147, he rejected another royal candidate and consecrated Henry Murdac as archbishop. Henry Murdac was at the time the abbot of the Cistercian abbey of Fountains, in Yorkshire, and a man well known to Bernard.

---

[20] Fawcett and Oram, 22.

# Abbot of Revesby

In 1143, William de Roumare, earl of Lincoln, founded Revesby abbey in Lindsey, twenty miles from Lincoln, and Rievaulx was chosen as the mother house of the new abbey.

A suitable location was chosen and the founder ensured that a church, refectory and other essential buildings were in place before the monks arrived. This will have been done in close consultation with Rievaulx's abbot and probably involved lay brothers in the construction work. It is strange that the Revesby was chosen as the location of the new abbey as it was not desolate and necessitated the destruction of three small villages.[21] The founder offered the inhabitants of the villages a choice of either new land or the freedom to go live where they wanted.[22] The Cistercian order provided copies of the Benedictine Rule, the Cistercian customs and service books and the first twelve monks and an abbot. The monk selected as the first abbot of Revesby was Aelred.

At Revesby, Aelred had the experience of developing a new foundation and soon became a well-known and respected figure in the area. Walter Daniel tells us that Aelred's fame spread throughout the whole countryside: bishops, earls, and barons venerated him and the new abbey, and in their reverence and affection made many donations and defended the abbey by their peace and protection. The bishop of Lincoln asked Aelred to preach at local church councils and also to assist in the reform of the clergy.[23]

---

[21] Squire, 32 (original source: Hoskins, W. G. The Making of the English Landscape, 1955, 81).
[22] Fergusson P. & Harrison, 64.
[23] Daniel, 28.

Walter Daniel very briefly gives us a window into how unsettled this time was when he writes about the acceptance of land donations from knights:

> "in this unsettled time such gifts profited knights and monks alike, for in those days it was hard for any to lead the good life unless they were monks or members of some religious order, so disturbed and chaotic was the land, reduced almost to a desert by the malice, slaughters and harryings of evil men".[24]

The problems caused by the ongoing dispute between Stephen and Matilda continued. Not all areas were affected at the same time as the battles focused on specific locations: a couple of years before Aelred's arrival at Revesby, Lincoln had suffered enormously and, shortly after his arrival, destruction and devastation swept the fens, south of Lincolnshire.

The suffering was widespread. Many people lost their lives and many of the survivors were made destitute overnight as fires swept through their homes, crops and businesses. The repercussions were felt across the country as displaced people moved from one area to another seeking safety and a way to make a living. It was not an easy time and many people died of starvation.

On 2 August 1145 William, the much-loved abbot of Rievaulx died. There will have been a great deal of sadness at Rievaulx and the daughter houses including Revesby. Whilst we know little about William we do know that he was immensely successful in developing Rievaulx and in securing its future. He was obviously a man of great personal integrity and charisma and the abbey and its monks thrived

---

24 Ibid., 28.

under his abbacy. Maurice, a respected member of the Rievaulx community, was chosen as his successor.

We do not know if Aelred travelled to Rievaulx at this time but it seems possible that he did to pay his respects and to take part in the election of the new abbot of Rievaulx. If he did, the visit will have been a brief one as he will have needed to set out for the Annual General Chapter in France. On his return he was kept busy with the development of Revesby and was probably also involved in the development of Rievaulx's latest daughter house at Rufford which was nearby.

The development of Rufford abbey led to the disappearance of three more villages, two of which became monastic granges. Some of the displaced people were settled in a new planned village named Wellow and others were given compensation ranging from 10 shillings to 20 pence.[25]

## The Second Crusade

During Aelred's time in Lincolnshire, Saracen rulers conquered Mesopotamia and, in 1144, captured Odessa. The threat to the fragile hold the first crusade had attained in the Holy Land led to Pope Eugenius III, on 1 March 1146, initiating the Second Crusade on God's behalf. At the request of the Pope and the French King, Bernard of Clairvaux preached in favour of the Second Crusade.

On 31 March 1146, visitors from all over France descended on Vézelay to hear Bernard preach. The crowd was too large to fit in the Cathedral so Bernard spoke to them from a platform erected in a field outside the town. His actual words are lost to us but we know that "he read out the papal Bull asking for a holy expedition" and promised

---

[25] Williams, D. H., 173, (from Cistercian Land Clearances by M. W. Barley).

absolution to all that took part in it.[26] It was by all accounts a very successful event with many men taking up the Cross and pledging themselves to the Crusade.

Encouraged by his success Bernard undertook a tour of Burgundy, Lorraine and Flanders preaching the crusade as he went. As had happened in the early days of the First Crusade, the crusading zeal led to attacks on Jews. In Germany, Rudolf, a fanatical Cistercian monk, was responsible for inspiring Jewish massacres and Bernard was summoned to deal with him, staying on in Germany to preach the crusade.[27] After Germany, he continued his travels throughout France supervising arrangements for the Crusade and writing to all European Cistercian houses requesting their support in promoting the crusade.

The preaching of war seems like a contradiction to the Cistercian belief system but there is always some form of justification when one side believes itself to be one hundred percent right. Bernard said he was not condoning war but that God had permitted Palestine to be conquered by non-believers so that Christians might fight for the Holy Land and by doing so gain complete remittance of their sins.[28] What did Aelred think about the Crusade? Did he preach in its favour? Sadly, we don't know. My own suspicion is that he will have been more preoccupied with his new role as abbot rather than with the promotion of the Crusade.

In 1147 the main body of the Crusade set out including amongst its numbers King Louis of France and his wife Eleanor of Aquitaine. Two years later, after many disasters, the crusade came to an unsuccessful end: Bernard glossed

---

26 Runciman, 253.
27 Ibid., 254.
28 Bulst-Thiele, 61.

over the failure by representing it as one of the mysterious ways in which God works.[29]

## Miracles and Cures

Walter Daniel tells us that Aelred was responsible for a number of miracles and cures during his time at Revesby. Three of these are outlined below.

The sub prior who had long suffered from "very sharp attacks of fever" became seriously ill. He lay on his bed "his limbs scarcely holding together, for the contraction and loosening of his joints and nerves made them leap from the sockets of his bones, and only the thin layer of fragile skin kept his body together".[30] On visiting the infirmary Aelred said to the man: "Tomorrow, in the name of the Lord, make your way to the church, take your place in the choir of the psalmodists, sing with them and pray to God, and through Him, I believe, you will be well". The monk did as instructed and his health was restored and with it a deeper faith and conviction in God.[31]

The unstable monk that we first met when Aelred was a novice master was one of the twelve monks that came to Revesby and whilst there threw another "wobble". He could not endure the daily tasks, the vigils were too long for him, the food was awful, the clothing was too rough and he longed for the delights of the world.[32] Aelred was prepared to help alleviate some of the pressures for him by allowing him better food and softer clothing as long as he stayed but the monk refused and was adamant that he was going to leave. Aelred, to the consternation of the other monks, vowed to

---

[29] Williams, D. H., 163.
[30] Daniel, 29.
[31] Ibid., 30.
[32] Ibid., 30.

fast until the unstable monk returned. The monk raced to leave the abbey, reached the gate, the doors were open but the air was like a "wall of iron". Again, and again he tried to pass through but without any success. Aelred's love had shut the air against him and, when his fury was spent, he calmed down and returned to ask for Aelred's pardon.[33]

One of the monks, "a skilled craftsman", seriously injured his arm. The severity of the injury had affected the whole limb and given it "a threefold twist back upon itself like a ram's horn, and paralysed and contorted the hand beneath".[34] Walter tells us that the monk had great faith and one day on his way into the church for Mass he noticed Aelred's staff by the door. He took the staff in his good hand and passed it "three times in a circle about the sick limb, making the sign of the Cross three times". By the time he had finished, his arm was restored to its usual position and mobility was restored to his hand.

## Monastic Expansion

From its early days, Christianity gave rise to the formation of communities dedicated to celibacy and the religious life. Before 1100 there were approximately 88 religious houses in England and Wales, by 1176 the number had increased to 340.[35] The dramatic increase in numbers was primarily due to foundations being developed by the new orders, most notably the Cistercians, Savignacs, Premonstratensians, and the Gilbertines.

Why did the twelfth century see such an enormous expansion of monasteries? What compelled men to found

---

33 Ibid., 31–32.
34 Ibid., 32.
35 Knowles, 711.

new orders and abbeys, and what compelled individuals to join them? There is no simple answer to any of these questions but we can allow ourselves some degree of speculation. Our starting point needs to be some understanding of how the Universe was viewed in the twelfth century.

The physical universe was believed to have a definite beginning and an end and the world was calculated to be five or six thousand years old. The figure was arrived at by using details from the bible including the life spans of the patriarchs. Because of text variations, the exact number of years varied. "Whatever their view of the exact date of Creation, most people presumed that the future would be shorter than the past."[36] This appears to have arisen from the belief that the world had six ages. The first five of these ran from the time of Creation to the time of Jesus when the sixth, and final, age began. Many felt that Judgement Day would arrive before the end of the twelfth century. There was a definite feeling that the end of the world must be nigh.

The other thing we have to remember is that belief in God was widespread and the church was a powerful and ever present force in people's lives. People wanted to be saved on judgement day and the quickest path to salvation was through a virtuous life. The easiest way of living a virtuous life was as a monk whether that be in community with other men or as a hermit. If you couldn't become a monk you could help your quest for eternal salvation by supporting monasteries. If you were poor, you could pray.

It wasn't just the monasteries that were growing, there was also an increase in the number of other religious buildings. William of Malmesbury wrote that, after the

---

[36] Bartlett, 655.

Norman Conquest, "everywhere you could see churches rising up in the villages and minsters in the towns and cities"[37]. Many of these ventures were not small: "Great new cathedral churches rose above the bishops' cities, eclipsing in scale and elegance those that had gone before."[38] It is likely that Aelred will have visited many of the new cathedrals whilst on his travels.

Over the years, Aelred had contact with members of all the different orders. Sometimes these contacts were of a practical nature regarding land ownership and sometimes these were of a spiritual nature. Lincolnshire saw the development of Gilbertine and Premonstratensian houses during Aelred's abbacy at Revesby.

Gilbert of Sempringham inherited two churches from his father but never intended to found a new order. His primary goal was to live simply and care well for those in his charge. After being approached by a small number of local women who were keen to follow a religious life he, with the help of Bishop Alexander of Lincoln, built a dwelling and cloister for the nuns against the north wall of his Sempringham church. Whilst Gilbert maintained his reluctance to develop the fledgling order, he went on to found double houses with the men following the Augustinian rule and the women that of St Benedict.

He received visits and advice from Abbot William of Rievaulx on the foundation of the Order and, further assistance, from the Cistercian Order in the late 1140s. The main Gilbertine base was in Lincolnshire and it is inevitable that the Gilbert and Aelred will have met on numerous occasions especially when Aelred was abbot of Revesby.

---

[37] Ibid., 386.
[38] Ibid., 391.

The Premonstratensians founded by Norbert in 1121, although based on the Augustinian rule, had many similarities with the Cistercians including the use of lay brothers, the institution of a general chapter, a preference for remote locations, manual labour and white robes. Peter of Goxhill, a Lincolnshire baron, founded a Premonstratensian abbey at Newhouse, the first of one hundred and thirty such houses in the country. Gerlo was made abbot and remained in office until his death in about 1165. Aelred will have come to know him well.

## Jews in England

Christianity was the religion that permeated everybody's lives but it was not the only faith in existence. Jews started arriving in England after the Norman Conquest and were already established under Stephen's reign. Most towns that served as trading centres had a settlement of Jews. They fulfilled a vital role which Christians were forbidden from engaging in—the lending of money for interest (usury). Their trading was not restricted to secular interests; many monasteries, the Cistercians included, borrowed money from Jews.

The power that money lending gave them, coupled with their different customs, dress and language, set them apart from the majority of the population making them unpopular and targets of hatred. They were often accused of crimes whether they were guilty or not: for example, in 1144, William, a twelve-year old Christian boy, was found murdered in a wood near his home in Norwich. His uncle, Godwin, insisted that his nephew had been murdered by Jews. It was a view that was accepted all too easily as there was a common belief in circulation that the Jews sacrificed a Christian somewhere each year and 1144 was assumed to be the year for Norwich. The boy was heralded a saint and over the next thirty years his body was translated a number of times, each time to a place of higher honour.

# Chapter 5

# Abbot of Rievaulx

By 1147 the Cistercians were at the height of their influence. The Catholic Church had its first Cistercian Pope. In England, Henry Murdac, from Fountains abbey, held the office of archbishop of York. The orders of Savigny and Sempringham wanted to join the Cistercians, the number of abbeys was ever increasing and more and more men were choosing to become Cistercian monks and lay brothers.

The General Chapter of 1147 was a historic meeting with the Pope in attendance. The Order of Savigny was incorporated but the request from Gilbert of Sempringham was denied—the Cistercians were a male only club and did not want responsibility for nunneries. There was discussion of the second crusade and various internal issues including the resignation of Maurice as Abbot of Rievaulx. The only recorded reason for his resignation was that he preferred the simplicity of life as a monk. It was a decision that was to change Aelred's life.

According to the Cistercian Rule, a Cistercian abbey could elect any white monk as its abbot but it was usually the case that the abbot was selected from within the abbeys own family—the mother house and any daughter houses.[1] Rievaulx, at this time was one of the most important religious houses in England, and the abbot, whoever he was, would be expected to play a significant role in secular and political affairs outside of the abbey—his opinion would be sought and his presence expected at certain events. Rievaulx's abbot needed to be a man of influence and the community decided that the right man for the job was Aelred. In the autumn of 1147, Aelred left Revesby and returned to Rievaulx. His earliest recorded public action as abbot of Rievaulx was on 30 November 1147, only a few weeks after his election, when he co-operated with Bishop William of Durham in an inquiry to settle a dispute about the seat of the prior at Durham.[2]

As abbot, Aelred was in charge of the spiritual direction of all his monks. He was also in charge of ensuring that the monks' physical needs were met and that the abbey had a sound economic basis. To do these he had to be involved in a wide range of "non-spiritual" activities including administration, inspecting monastic granges, witnessing charters, liaising with existing and new benefactors, meeting with abbey visitors, and planning for Rievaulx's future. Alongside these tasks, Aelred was also expected to participate in the usual routines of the day, leading the brethren in work and devotion. Aelred also wrote and preached.

---

[1] Burton, 164.
[2] Daniel: Powicke, introduction, xci.

King David's household had provided Aelred with a sound training ground for learning how to deal with a wide variety of people from different backgrounds and, as steward, he had developed organisational and, most importantly, diplomatic skills. The fact that Aelred was so well loved by his monks shows that he had the ability to hear and value each individual. He had embraced the Cistercian philosophy of equality but he also understood that each monk had different skills and abilities, and strengths and weaknesses. He had high expectations of his monks but his success as an abbot came from an understanding of men's weaknesses.

Building work at Rievaulx acquired a further spurt of momentum during Aelred's time as abbot. Fergusson and Harrison discuss in detail the role Aelred may have played in the design and architecture of the abbey, speculating on influences from both France and Italy.[3] What we do know is that Aelred immediately embarked on plans to extend the abbey to accommodate the increasing numbers of new recruits. This was not a straightforward process as Rievaulx abbey has a river on one side and hills on the other but neither of these stopped the expansion. The church that Abbot William had built was demolished and excavations were made into the hillside to accommodate a larger church.[4]

The early 1150s saw the development of a new Chapter House, bigger and grander than the one originally built by William. It was a chapter house that resembled no other chapter house either within the Cistercian Order or outside it:[5] it had an ambulatory around the outside that was

---

[3] Fergusson P. & Harrison, 59–68.
[4] Ibid., 69.
[5] Ibid., 66.

separated from the main building by large circular piers.[6]
Other construction included the East Nave, a latrine block,
new novice quarters and an Infirmary which was adapted, in
the mid to late 1150s, to accommodate a residence
specifically for Aelred as an abbot with health problems. It
seems likely that the major work was completed by 1160
when Rievaulx received a papal bull recognising the abbey's
privileges—a type of document that was often acquired to
coincide with the completion of major work.[7]

# Aelred's Management Team

It would have been impossible for Aelred to carry out all the
activities necessary for a smoothly functioning abbey on his
own. There were a number of key positions, below his as
abbot, that were vital to the success of Rievaulx.

The official next in importance to Aelred was the Prior.
The prior's main role was the overall supervision of internal
arrangements and discipline within the abbey: "He was
required to come into a much more intimate and familiar
relation with the other members of the community than was
the abbot. He was their counsellor, their guide, their helper
in all matters of religious observance. On every occasion
when the abbot was absent from the monastery, discharging
parliamentary or other duty, the prior took his place as the
superior and wielded his authority".[8] The next official of
importance was the sub-prior who assisted the prior in his
duties and acted in his place should he have to be absent
from the abbey.

---

6 Tatton-Brown T, Crook, 110.
7 Fergusson P. & Harrison, 130.
8 Christie, 23.

The Precentor was responsible for "making arrangements for the proper conduct of worship". He selected the music, chose the singers, and was responsible for training the monks in "the due discharge of their choir duties". Given the amount of time the monks spent in church each day, the office of Precentor was a key role.[9] The Sacrist took care of the church: "He saw that it was kept clean and tidy, that its furniture was all rightly placed, that the altars were suitably dressed, that the vessels of the sanctuary were duly cared for, and that the appropriate vestments were laid out for the use of the priests who needed them in any particular service." The Sacrist was also responsible for the lighting of the whole monastery, and for looking after the monks' cemetery.[10]

The Cellarer had the feeding of the community as his chief responsibility: "He had to see that sufficient food was provided to supply the needs of the brethren."[11] He was also responsible for the work and discipline of the lay brothers, aided by the grangers, and as such served as the business manager of the monastery.[12] The Kitchener was responsible for the daily preparation of all the meals.[13] Then there was the Refectorian who was "charged with the responsibility of attending to the refectory or dining-hall, and having all things in readiness for the community when they came to partake of their meals."[14]

Sick and elderly monks lived in the infirmary. All activities in the infirmary including medical care, diet, physical care, organisation and administration, fell under the supervision of the Infirmarer: "Part of the duty assigned to

---

[9] Christie, 23–6.
[10] Ibid., 23–6, 269.
[11] Ibid., 23–6.
[12] Williams, D. H., 85.
[13] Christie, 23–6.
[14] Ibid., 23–6.

him was that of bleeding the monks, an operation which was considered to be good for their health, and to which they had to submit themselves four times each year."[15]

The Almoner was responsible for the good works and charity of the monastery: for example, he "gathered together all that was left after dinner had been served to the monks, and distributed it to the poor with whatever other portion might have been specially allotted for such a purpose."[16] The Chamberlain was responsible for looking after "the monks wardrobe".[17] There was also a Master of Novices and a Master of the Lay Brethren. The latter was responsible for overseeing the lay brothers of the abbey,[18] and acted as their spiritual director and confessor.[19] As many of the books in Rievaulx's Library will have been copied in the abbey, someone will have been appointed as supervisor of the scribes in whatever passed as the scriptorium.[20]

Abbeys provided hospitality to wayfarers, travellers, pilgrims, benefactors, and merchants. A guesthouse, set at a distance from the main abbey buildings, was built to accommodate these visitors and was under the control of the abbey's Guest Master.[21] The abbey's Gatehouse was the immediate point of contact between the abbey and the outside world and a wide range of people arrived at its doors including potential monks, pilgrims, refugees, people who were ill and seeking medical help, the old looking for help, servants looking for work, relatives of the monks,

---

[15] Ibid., 23–6.
[16] Ibid., 23–6.
[17] Ibid., 23–6.
[18] Ibid., 23–6.
[19] Williams, D. H., 85.
[20] Ibid., 101.
[21] Christie, 23–6.

benefactors, neighbours, travellers and those seeking sanctuary.[22]

For practical purposes, the majority of the poor received their alms at the door and were not admitted. For the others, the gatehouse keeper had to make a decision as to whether he admitted them or not. His role was as a key one and it required a certain kind of individual to carry out his work. The Gatehouse was such a key element of the abbey that the Cistercian Rule included the Gatekeeper's cell as one of the first buildings to be constructed.

Unlike the other monks, the gatekeeper slept near the gate so that callers could be dealt with as soon as possible: he was "almoner, businessman, watch-man and gaoler".[23] He would receive guests and callers with a cry of *Deo gratias.* The genuine visitors he would admit with a genuflexion and notify Aelred. If Aelred approved the guests, they were handed over to the guest master who was responsible for deciding what and when they ate, and where they slept.[24] Guesthouses were quite large and, going on Walter Daniels account, the one at Rievaulx had several rooms[25]—a necessary feature to accommodate the differing ranks of people.

## Walter Daniel

Three years into Aelred's abbacy, Walter Daniel, Aelred's future biographer, joined Rievaulx. Apparently, Aelred brought Walter Daniel to Rievaulx after one of his visits to

---

[22] Williams, D. H., 115, 125.
[23] Ibid., 118.
[24] Ibid., 125.
[25] Daniel, 73.

Durham.[26] Walter Daniel's father was already a monk at Rievaulx, probably one of its officials.[27]

Thomas Merton describes Walter as one of Aelred's "precocious intellectuals".[28] He had received an education and was licensed to teach and, whilst at Rievaulx, he became a prolific writer.[29] Interestingly his education was more formal than Aelred's but his writings were lacking in the insights gained from direct spiritual experience that are so evident in Aelred's works.[30] Aelred wrote from the heart and from his own spiritual understanding in a way that Walter was never able to emulate.

As Walter seems very familiar with medical terms it is often speculated that he was the infirmarer at Rievaulx which, given Aelred's failing health, meant he had the opportunity to spend more time with his abbot than most. However, Walter makes mention of Aelred entrusting the "care of his illness entirely to the ministrations of two of the brethren"[31] and he does not say that one of them was himself. He also states that Aelred's writings were "preserved for prosperity by the labour of my own hand"[32] and this comment leads me to think that Walter, rather than being the infirmarer, was Aelred's secretary, at least, in the last few years.

During the last four years of Aelred's life, Walter describes the way Aelred avoided taking "curatives". It seems that his carers tried to slip these into his food and Aelred if he tasted "anything of that kind in his mouth" took

---

[26] Merton, IV, 56.
[27] Daniel: Powicke, introduction, xii.
[28] Merton, IV, 56.
[29] Daniel: Powicke, introduction, xvii–xviii
[30] Merton, IV, 57.
[31] Daniel, 39.
[32] Ibid., 27.

it out with his fingers and, while his attendants were engaged on other things, "threw it on the ground and ground it to powder with his foot so that it should not be seen".[33] If Walter had been the infirmarer I would have expected him to explain how these curatives would have helped Aelred and also to have mentioned how he himself had tried to give them to Aelred yet he doesn't—he describes the episodes as an observer and never as a participant. He also tells us that Aelred "taking his soul in his hands, gave greater weight to his own counsels than to those of the physicians and for God's sake despised the cure of the body and considered in all ways the health of the soul".[34] Given Walter's personality I would have expected him to be "put-out" by Aelred's views and actions if he had been the infirmarer.

Walter's knowledge of the details of Aelred's illnesses could simply be that he was often with Aelred. It seems unlikely that Aelred will have wanted constant fussing by a nurse or doctor but a secretary, who could help with the writing of his books as well as abbey correspondence, would have been welcome. It is also the case that Aelred will not have always needed Walter's assistance as secretary and as monks were not allowed "down-time" Walter will have had at least one other role within the abbey which could have been in the infirmary.

There is a further instance in Walter Daniel's biography that indicates a secretarial role. In the case of the dying monk, Walter tells us that Aelred is sitting in the orchard, transacting certain business with the cellarers when news arrives from the infirmary that a monk with heart failure has taken a turn for the worse and is dying. Walter insists that he

[33] Ibid., 49.
[34] Ibid., 49–50.

was with Aelred when the news arrived.[35] I cannot see that an infirmarer would have been needed at such a meeting, and given that Aelred was able to make his way unaided (without even his staff) to the monk would imply that he didn't need physical assistance on that day. I am pretty certain that Walter had been taking notes as, surely, if he had been the infirmarer he would known about the monk's condition and, given the severity of the situation, would have been in the infirmary at that time.

## Change, Peace, and Sadness

The conflict between Stephen and Matilda had never fully ceased but it was brought to an end when, in 1152, Stephen's eldest son and proposed heir, Eustace, died. As his other son expressed no interest in following in his father's footsteps, Stephen declared Matilda's son, Henry, as his successor.

In June 1152, King David's only son, Henry died and was buried at Kelso.[36] As Henry had been prepared and schooled for the role of King, his death had serious implications for Scotland. The next in line to the Scottish throne was David's grandson, Malcolm, who was still a young boy. To avoid potential problems, David arranged for Malcolm to be presented to his future subjects as the designated heir. On his tour of Scotland, Donchad, the Earl of Fife, who David had elected as the boy's guardian, accompanied him.[37]

For Aelred, 1153 was a year of massive change and a great deal of personal loss. During Lent of that year, Aelred visited Scotland to discuss the needs of Rievaulx with King David. Aelred describes it as "some urgent need of our

---

35 Ibid., 43.
36 Barrow, 1981, 42.
37 Oram, 2008, 200-01.

house"[38] but there is no information available as to what these discussions actually involved but they must have been of some importance for Aelred to have undertaken travel during lent. Soon after this visit, on 24 May at Carlisle, King David died.

## Lament for King David

At some point in 1153, Aelred wrote his *Lament for David* that is often included as an introduction to his *Genealogy of the Kings* but I doubt that it was originally intended for this purpose. The lament is a beautiful piece of writing that describes King David over the years, both his positive attributes and his failings. Aelred writes:

> "We have lost a man who lived not for himself but for everyone, caring for everyone, providing for the welfare of everyone: a teacher of morals, an examiner of crimes, an encourager of virtues... His gentleness made him lovable, his justice made him fearsome, his chastity made him calm, his humility made him accessible."[39]

David had brought Scotland together, promoted religious houses, looked after the poor and made himself available to all. He did make some errors in his life but he was, overall, always a just and fair King and much loved by his people. Aelred's grief is evident in the piece and his descriptions of David have been used by many historians over the years as there is sadly very little other information available about David's life.

---

[38] Aelred: Lament for David, 58.
[39] Ibid., 45–46.

During his Lenten visit, Aelred describes David as living the life of a monk: "I found in the king a monk, a cloister in the court, in the palace the discipline of a monastery".[40] David attended services, set time aside for prayer and reading of the psalms, and time each day for service to the poor. He also spent some time each day apparently gardening. He consulted with his religious advisors and toward the end of each day dealt with official business. What I find most intriguing is the amount of detail the lament contains about the last days of David's death.

Aelred tells us that on Wednesday 20 May King David began to prepare his advisors and himself for his death. The detail of the activities of these next few days, especially the last two before his death on the following Monday, must indicate that Aelred spoke to some of the individuals involved very soon after David's death. For example, we know that David was too ill to stand or walk on the Saturday but insisted on receiving communion at the altar and was carried there by monks and soldiers. He asked to see the "black cross" which was a clever box designed in the shape of a cross that contained part of Jesus' cross and had been handed down to him by his mother (St. Margaret). Whilst receiving the last rites he corrected the clergy present for chanting too fast as he wanted to focus on each and every word of the psalms. We know he instructed his household that news of his death must be given immediately after it happened. We know that on the Sunday he was reflecting on certain Psalms and he checked with his clerk Nicholas that alms had been given to the poor that day.

The account is so real, so present, that Aelred must have been told the details very soon after David died. Could

---

40 Ibid., 58.

Aelred have still been in the area somewhere? We know that David died in Carlisle and that his body was taken to Dunfermline for burial in the abbey alongside other family members.[41] It is likely that Aelred's visit with David in Lent was in Carlisle. It also seems likely that he then went onto Dundrennan and then to Melrose. It is entirely possible that he was still in Scotland or on his way south maybe at Durham or Hexham when he received the news and returned north. I know that stories were preserved orally in a way that they are no longer but there is an immediacy to the account that implies it was written down very soon after the death.

It is pure speculation on my part but I suspect that Aelred may have been present during King David's last days. If the news had reached him of David's failing health he could have easily returned to Carlisle in time and his presence would explain the wealth of detail that the Lament contains. Logic would dictate that if Aelred had been an eyewitness that he would have said so but there were sound political reasons for this not to have been mentioned. Aelred loved and respected David—he had been his mentor and benefactor in his youth and their relationship had continued over the years. However, as abbot of Rievaulx, Aelred's allegiance always had to be to the English King. To protect Rievaulx's interests, and the reputation of the Cistercians, Aelred could not be seen to do anything that would question this loyalty. It is quite reasonable, therefore, that if Aelred had been present when David died that he did not proclaim this action publicly. Realistically, most people will have known he had been present but some things were best left unwritten.

---

[41] Oram, 2008, 202.

## More Deaths

On 8 July 1153 Pope Eugenius died, followed by Bernard of Clairvaux on 20 August.[42] Walter Espec, Rievaulx's founder and patron, retired to Rievaulx in 1153 where he remained until his death in 1155.

Henry Murdac, the Cistercian archbishop of York, also died in 1153 and, without the opposition of Eugenius or Bernard, William Fitzherbert was reinstated as archbishop of York. He was apparently welcomed back to York by a vast crowd of people so big that one of the bridges over the river Ouse collapsed. No one died in the accident and this "escape from death" was attributed to William's holiness. He was, however, not able to enjoy his role for long as on 8 June 1154 he also died. His replacement was Roger de Pont L'Evêque. Roger was to bring about major changes to York Minster including the construction of a new choir and crypt and the addition of two western towers.

## Genealogy of the Kings

Aelred completed his *Genealogy of the Kings* by mid 1154. It is addressed to Henry as Duke of Normandy and must have been undertaken after Stephen's agreement to have Henry succeed him. Its purpose was to outline kingship and Aelred confines himself to the Christian kings of England whose footsteps Henry would follow. He traces Henry's ancestry through his mother, her maternal grandmother (St Margaret of Scotland), and then back through time until he reaches Adam, the father of all men.

The qualities he outlines for Henry include mercy, chastity, humility, patronage of the church, generosity,

---

[42] Bredero, 286.

respect for the clergy and justice. He explores some of the
kings, including "the very devout King Alfred" and "King
Edgar the Peaceful" in some detail outlining the main events
of their lives and, more importantly, their qualities.[43] The
timing of the book was perfect as on 25 October 1154 King
Stephen died and Henry II became King of England. After
nearly twenty years of constant battles and feuds, peace
began to return to the country.

Exactly why Aelred wrote the *Genealogy of the Kings* is
somewhat of a mystery. Did he, out of concern for peace and
stability for the country, choose to do it himself or did
someone ask him to write it? My suspicion is that it was the
latter but I have no evidence. Maybe the powers that be were
a little tired of Geoffrey of Monmouth's history with all its
romance of Arthur and wanted something, by a respected
individual, to take its place, a more "real" history rather
than just a story. It was definitely the case that Henry of
Anjou, as King of England, was seen as a king who could
reconcile the English and Norman traditions. He was also
the first king since the Conquest who could claim to be
descended from Alfred.

## Battle of the Standard

At some point between 1155 and 1157 Aelred wrote his tract
on the Battle of the Standard.[44] This work, his genealogy of
the English Kings and his later biography of Edward the
Confessor are concerned with issues of national identity and
were most likely written with Henry II in mind.

One does have to ask why he embarked on an account of
the Battle of the Standard so many years after its event. It is

---

[43] Aelred: Genealogy of the Kings.
[44] Aelred: Battle of the Standard.

possible that the battle itself is of little significance to him except as a vehicle for illustrating the problems faced by a king (David) who must govern a wide diversity of men. In David's case these included Galloway men who were said to be particularly barbaric. I agree with Powicke when he writes that: "As a piece of historical writing its value is due to the understanding of events rather than to the accuracy of the narrative."[45]

Aelred is keen to demonstrate that understanding followed by forgiveness can be achieved by analysing difficulties. The work could also be viewed as a veiled commentary on the reign of Stephen who was seen as being pleasant and affable but a weak ruler lacking in resolution and decisiveness. It presents a fascinating account of how whilst on opposite sides in this battle there had been a great deal of friendship and links between both sides as is the case with Walter Espec, Robert de Brus and Bernard de Balliol all of whom had been friends with David.

## Whithorn

Aelred wrote his *Life of St Ninian* for the clergy and people of the Whithorn area in Scotland probably to coincide with the consecration of Christian as bishop of Whithorn on 19 December 1154. The request probably originated with Fergus, the first Lord of Galloway who had re-established the see at Whithorn and was also the founder of Rievaulx's daughter house at Dundrennan.

The *Life of Ninian* is quite a short piece of writing that recounts the main events known about St Ninian's life. We learn how Ninian sought true Christian teachings in Rome and how he was sent, as a confirmed bishop, to found a

---

[45] Daniel: Powicke, introduction, xlv.

church at Whithorn. Aelred outlines details of the some of the miracles that have been credited to Ninian and those that took place after his death, including the healing of two lepers.[46] We do not know if Aelred attended the consecration ceremony but he will surely have been invited.

# Visits and Travels

In his role as abbot, Aelred was frequently away from Rievaulx. His journeys included visits to daughter houses, the Cistercian Annual General Chapter, Rievaulx's granges, benefactors, kings, archbishops, and bishops. He was, also, called upon to witness charters, to settle disputes, to preach, to attend dedication ceremonies and to represent Rievaulx, and the Cistercians, at various events. He will also have had contact with various monasteries, abbeys and priories from other orders. For example, in 1150, Gilbertine houses were established at Old Malton and Watton in Yorkshire. Given Aelred's Lincolnshire connections with Gilbert he will have visited these at some point.

Aelred spent many months each year on the road Visits to daughter houses, granges and the annual general chapter took place each year and will have provided some degree of structure to Aelred's travel itinerary.

## Travel in the Twelfth Century

There is very little information on travel generally and road locations in the twelfth century.[47] No maps exist from that era and the details of journeys recorded in books written at the time, usually only tell us that someone went from, say,

---

46 Aelred: Ninian.
47 Stenton, M. D., 234–52.

Lincoln to York, without giving details of how they did it or where they stopped on route. The earliest maps we have are a series of four drawn by Matthew Paris, a monk of St Albans, in about 1250.[48]

The paucity of available information has led to speculation that travel was minimal but that was not the case. Travel in the twelfth century was frequent and, from the perspective of people living then, was no more difficult than travel is for us today. They faced different hazards than we do but if they had to get to a certain destination, whether it was because of business, politics, leisure or religion, they made the journey—people from all strata of society were on the move.

Travel was by foot, horse or boat and travellers, regardless of the length of their journey, were always at the mercy of the weather. Late spring, summer and early autumn were the easiest times for travelling; the days were longer and warmer, food was more readily available for both men and horses and the roads and rivers were more passable.[49] Travel did not, however, grind to a halt in the winter months; it just wasn't as safe or as comfortable and, because of the lack of daylight hours, could take much longer.

People travelled by water and by road and debate as to which was more prevalent seems a little irrelevant. Both methods were used and they will have been used according to the nature of the journey, the destination, the cost, the length of the journey, and how quickly one needed to arrive. By today's standards, travel was slow. On foot a man could cover between two and a half and four miles an hour so could conceivably travel between twenty and twenty-five

---

48 Hindle, 2009, 31.
49 Ohler, 3–14.

miles a day.[50] On horseback, a traveller could cover between thirty and forty miles a day which was obviously far faster than walking but expensive. On long journeys it was also essential to factor in rest days for both men and horses.

Aelred was an accomplished horse rider and we know that many of his journeys were on horseback. The only journeys Aelred is likely to have undertaken on foot will have been to locations very near to Rievaulx, such as a grange or, possibly, Byland Abbey or Helmsley Castle. Whilst austerity was a key element of the Cistercian way of life, travel on foot to all the places Aelred needed to reach would have meant he was continuously away from Rievaulx and so was never an option open to him. Aelred will not have been allowed to travel alone: he will always have had at least two companions with him: a secretary monk, and a lay brother to look after the horses.

## Daughter Houses

The annual visits to daughter houses were an important part of the Cistercian order. St Benedict's rule assumed each abbey would be autonomous but the Cistercians were concerned about preserving standards and ensuring uniformity in obedience to the rule. Their solution was a system by which the abbeys would be autonomous but with internal policing.

In practice, this meant that each abbey was responsible for overseeing the conduct of its own daughter foundations and this was carried out by an annual visit of the abbot of the mother house. The role of the visiting abbot was "simply to see that the Rule and the statutes of the general chapter

---

[50] Ohler, 97.

were being observed".[51] He was not supposed to interfere or undermine the authority of the abbot. If there were problems that needed to be addressed these were dealt with in consultation with other abbots.

Aelred had five daughter houses to visit: Melrose and Dundrennan in Scotland, Revesby and Rufford in Lincolnshire, and Warden in Bedfordshire. It is likely that Aelred visited the Scottish daughter houses in early spring, after Lent, and caught up with the southern houses of Rufford, Revesby and Warden whilst on route to or from the annual general chapter in September, but this is purely speculation as there are no records of when these visits took place.

## Melrose and Dundrennan

The first major stopping point for Aelred on a journey north to Scotland will have been Durham. It was around seventy miles to Durham from Rievaulx so Aelred's journey will have taken two days on horseback.

As Rievaulx's granges and estates extended north as far as Middleton in Teesdale, it seems likely that Aelred's first night was spent at one of these. He will then have been able to reach Durham, probably via Croft where there was a crossing over the river Tees, on the second day. Given his family links with the area and the important political and religious links with Durham's bishop and Cathedral, Aelred is likely to have stayed for at least a couple of days. We know that on at least one of his trips to Durham he visited the hermit Godric at Finchale.[52]

---

51 Lawrence, 188.
52 Rice, 205–207.

The journey from Durham to Melrose will then have taken a further two or three days. One of the routes that Aelred could have taken was to travel from Durham to Hexham his home town and, therefore, a logical place for him to visit. He could have stayed at the priory or even possibly with relatives. Then, he and his party could have travelled a further day north to Rochester and, on the following day, directly to Melrose.

An annual visit to Melrose will have been an opportunity for Aelred to maintain links and contacts with the Scottish monarchy—King David's castle at Roxburgh was only about 15 miles away. Aelred is likely to have stayed at Melrose for at least a week and included visits to other abbeys in the area such as Kelso, Dryburgh, and Jedburgh. The Tironensian abbey at Kelso was one of the richest and most influential in Scotland. As a visiting dignitary to the area it would have been politic for Aelred to pay his respects. The abbey owned property throughout Scotland, from Ayr to Aberdeenshire,[53] and during Aelred's time there were two key abbots: Herbert from 1127 to 1147, and Ernald from 1147 to 1160. Herbert was made bishop of Glasgow in 1147, and Ernald bishop of St Andrews in 1160.[54] The latter appointment was a significant event for the church and the state in Scotland and England; the King of Scotland and the papal legate attended the consecration ceremony, held at Dunfermline on 13 Nov 1160. It is exactly the type of event that Aelred would have been invited to attend.

Whilst it makes sense that Aelred continued his travels onto Dundrennan after visiting Melrose, it is difficult to establish the route he took. There are very few routes, even today, providing direct access across the border region of

---

[53] Baldwin, 163.
[54] Morton, 79–81.

Scotland and we have virtually no information about the situation in the twelfth century. We can only be sure that routes did exist and that they had to take into account the various rivers in the area.[55] If Aelred was going directly to Dundrennan, the route that suggests itself is Melrose to Moffat, via Selkirk, and then onto Dundrennan via Dumfries. It seems possible that the journey could have been made in two to three days.

Whilst in the Dundrennan area Aelred, on some occasions will have visited Kirkcudbright, just a few miles down the road,[56] and Whithorn, a day away on horseback. Fergus of Galloway, Dundrennan's patron, had one of his strongholds at Cruggleton just a few miles away from Whithorn and we know Aelred had contacts with him over the years so it is more than likely that he stayed at Cruggleton on at least one occasion.

His return journey to Rievaulx will have taken him to Carlisle but the journey is likely to have been too long to complete in a single day, a stopover will have been necessary possibly at Annan. The control of Carlisle and its castle changed hands from the British to the Scots on a number of occasions during Aelred's lifetime but, as an influential abbot, he was probably welcomed by both sides equally. As Hexham was only a day's ride away from Carlisle, Aelred probably completed the return journey by going to Hexham, Durham and then onto Rievaulx via one of the abbey's granges.

Aelred's involvement with daughter houses, at times, will have extended beyond just the annual visit. For example, in 1148, he had the onerous task of removing Richard as abbot

---

[55] Inglis.
[56] Daniel: Powicke, introduction, xciv.

of Melrose.[57] It seems that Richard had been too severe with the monks and that some of his methods had led to dissatisfaction and unease within the community. Waldef was selected to take his place.[58]

## Revesby, Rufford, and Warden

Revesby and Rufford, in Lincolnshire, are relatively close to each other (only 54 modern day miles), and. Warden, in Bedfordshire, is between 80 and 100 miles from either of the Lincolnshire abbeys. It seems logical that Aelred visited all three abbeys whilst travelling to and from Cîteaux for the annual general chapter perhaps spending time in the Lincolnshire ones on the way down and then at Warden on the return journey.

The starting point of all Aelred's southern journeys is most likely to have been York. A route down from Helmsley via Grimston Grange would have been just under thirty miles and easily completed in a day. In the same way as staying at Durham was politic, York, as the home of one of England's most important archbishops, was an essential stopping point. One of the routes suggested for travelling down to Lincolnshire is by horseback to Howden, by river along the Ouse to its junction with the Trent, along the Trent to Burton Stather and then by road to Lincoln.[59] Whilst this is a logical route if the destination is Lincoln I suspect that Aelred's first stop was probably one of the daughter houses. If this was the case, it would have been more logical to do the journey on horseback from York to Pontefract via

---

57 Fawcett and Oram, 22.
58 Merton, IV, 55.
59 Stenton, M. D., 251.

Tadcaster, Towton and Ferrybridge. Rufford abbey was then only another day's ride away.

After visiting Rufford, Aelred could conceivably have travelled onto Lincoln, for yet another diplomatic stopover and then Revesby was an easy day's ride away. To begin the long journey down to the south coast Aelred could then have visited his friend Gilbert of Hoyland, at Swineshead, which was less than 18 miles away. His next stopping point could have been Sempringham a further 12 miles away. We know that Abbot William, Aelred's predecessor, stayed with Gilbert of Sempringham whilst on journeys south.[60] As Gilbert was well known to Aelred it seems reasonable to suggest that Sempringham was a stopping point for him. The next logical stopping point would have been Sawtry abbey, a daughter house of Warden, and about 38 miles away from Sempringham. Warden itself was then only 30 miles away.

Whilst in this area, either as abbot of Revesby or when travelling from Rievaulx, Aelred must surely have visited some of the key sites of pilgrimage in the area including Walsingham and Thetford. It also seems more than likely that he was familiar with the cathedrals at Ely and Peterborough.

## Cistercian General Chapter

The Cistercian General Chapter met every year at Cîteaux on the vigil of Holy Cross Day, 13 September. The president of the Chapter Meeting was the Abbot of Cîteaux and the primary function of the meeting was to maintain observance of the Cistercian Rule.

The Chapter received reports, imposed penalties on abbots, reiterated existing regulations, discussed major issues

---

[60] Knowles, 205.

of the day, drew up new regulations and authorised new foundations.[61] It was also an opportunity for abbots to discuss with other abbots the day-to-day problems of managing an abbey.

The meetings themselves lasted from seven to ten days and the logistics of housing, feeding and organising the increasing number of abbots must have presented a major challenge to the Cîteaux community. In 1120 there were about 12 abbots, in 1130 there were about 40, and by 1150 there were around 300.[62] The ever-increasing numbers led to each abbot being restricted to only two travelling companions—a monk secretary and a lay brother.[63] If all the abbots, with their travelling companions, had turned up in 1150, Cîteaux would have been playing host to around 900 people.

The original egalitarian ideal of the general chapter was affected by the success of the Cistercians. There were quite simply too many abbots to be involved in every single discussion so a steering committee of twenty-five abbots was set up to hear cases and make decisions. In effect the committee controlled the way the general chapter functioned by deciding the agenda and bringing decisions forward for ratification and subsequent relaying to all Cistercians.

As the Order grew, it became difficult for the General Chapter to deal with a lot of the smaller issues concerning all the abbeys and after 1152 they took the decision that abbots of a mother house would visit all daughter houses once a year.[64] As Bernard died in 1153, this probably explains why there is no recorded visit at Rievaulx from Bernard as abbot

---

[61] Lawrence, 190.
[62] William, D. H., 35.
[63] Lawrence, 190.
[64] William, D. H., 41.

of Rievaulx's mother house, Clairvaux. Whilst Bernard undertook long journeys across Europe, there is no record of him having crossed the sea to England.[65]

The Cistercian founders never anticipated such rapid development over the whole of Europe. It seemed that each month brought news of a new foundation leading to the general chapter of 1152 forbidding the establishment of further foundations. Despite the problems that were involved in the organising and functioning of a body such as the general chapter it was successful enough to attract a great deal of attention and be copied by other orders. It is worth noting that in the twelfth century, the Cistercians had founded an organisation that transcended country boundaries—one of the first international assemblies within Europe.

Day one of the Annual General Chapter was taken up with the reading of the statutes and of any letters received. On the second day, after examination of faults and before Sext, representative abbots known as the "definitors" were appointed. The third day included sermons and prayers for the dead and then they got down to the business of looking into any shortcomings within the Order and discussing petitions of various kinds. Between sessions, the definitors drafted the Chapter's response.

On the last day, after prayers for earthly rulers and protectors, the agreed statutes were promulgated and the abbots started to disperse.[66] The abbots each took away with them a copy of all the decisions and were expected to make these known to all of their monks. These new statutes were

---

[65] Ibid., 3.
[66] Ibid., 33.

Cistercian law and there was no system of appeal allowed not even to the Pope.[67]

The General Chapter was an exciting time for many of those visiting and in the earlier years was quite a light-hearted event to the extent that the Chapter issued a statute prohibiting the abbots from "wandering gaily around the nearby city of Dijon arm in arm".[68] Many of the early abbots will have known each other having started out as monks at Clairvaux and some of the other French foundations.

In 1155, the Cistercian General Chapter instructed Aelred to make a decision as to whether Byland Abbey was to be classed as a daughter house of Furness or Savigny.[69] It is likely that, to ensure all sides had a fair hearing, that Aelred travelled to both Savigny, probably immediately after the General Chapter, and at a later point to Furness. His ruling was in favour of Savigny and it is a decision that will have pleased the monks of Byland as relations between Furness and Byland had become somewhat strained.

The journey from the North of England to Cîteaux took around four to five weeks. The first stage was to travel to the port, possibly Dover, around 300 miles away from Rievaulx, then across the channel, and through France to Cîteaux, approximately a further 380 miles away. It is no wonder that some abbots simply didn't go. In later years the rules were relaxed so that abbots from some areas, including Scotland, only had to attend once in every four years with a representative attending in the intervening years. We have no idea how many times Aelred made the journey but it could have been more than twenty times.

---

[67] Ibid., 33.
[68] Merton, V, 57.
[69] Burton, 290.

The previous section outlined a possible route from Rievaulx to Warden in Bedfordshire. From Warden we have to suppose that Aelred's destination was London where the English Cistercian abbots usually met together before setting of in convoy, not later than mid August.[70] They stayed at abbeys and granges on route but as to which these were would be pure speculation. One set of options that Aelred could have used is outlined below.

- St Albans, a popular Cathedral city and place of pilgrimage, was just over 30 miles away from Warden.
- Then the Cistercian abbey of Stratford Langthorne in London, about 26 miles away.
- Then onto the Cistercian abbey of Boxley in Kent (only from the mid 1140s), about thirty miles away.
- Then just under thirty miles away is Canterbury with its historic Cathedral and links to St Augustine.
- And, finally, about 18 miles on to the port of Dover.

We don't know if Dover was the port used but it is a prime candidate. One assumes that the Cistercian abbots from across England, Wales and Scotland joined together along the way and that the crossing to France was done as a large group.

In his book on medieval travel, Ohler states that, when on route to the annual general chapter at Cîteaux, many "Cistercian abbots travelled with a great retinue, accompanied by armed servants".[71] As the number of Cistercian abbeys increased, the General Chapter introduced

---

[70] Williams, D. H., 37.
[71] Ohler, 56.

a ruling that limited the number of companions an abbot could bring with him to a secretary monk and a lay brother. The idea of a "great retinue" probably arises from the simple fact that abbots travelled together. In respect of the British abbeys, in 1135 there would have been 5 abbots, in 1145 the number had increased to 22, and in 1165 there were 57. If each abbot had two travelling companions, the number crossing the channel and travelling through France together, in 1165, would have been greater than 165. Abbots from other parts of Europe will have also made similar travelling arrangements. It is also totally conceivable that some of their patrons insisted on armed escorts.

Once the English abbots arrived in France they probably made their way down to Rheims, 167 miles away, staying at Cistercian abbeys and granges on the way. From Rheims they will have continued onto Troyes, 77 miles away. We know that Aelred preached at Troyes—at least two sermons exist but without dates.[72] Henry of Carinthia was bishop of Troyes at the same time Aelred was Abbot of Rievaulx, he had formerly been a Cistercian monk and abbot so it is not surprising that he invited a well-known visiting abbot from his order to preach.[73] Having said that, Troyes pretty much had their pick of a multitude of Cistercian abbots that will have passed their way and Aelred is unlikely to have been the only one invited to preach there.

Clairvaux, Bernard's abbey, was only 40 miles south of Troyes and will have been the next stopping point; it was then only a further 94 miles to Cîteaux. And, of course, after the general chapter, the journey was repeated in reverse. Unexpected delays on the journey to the chapter could result in abbots arriving after the meeting had taken place so time

---

[72] Aelred: Spiritual Friendship; Roby, introduction, 11.
[73] Squire, 65.

must have been built in to account for the unexpected and it is not unreasonable to suppose that on some occasions delays were so severe that the journeys were cancelled. On one occasion, rough weather prevented the abbots from making the sea crossing, on the homeward journey, for two weeks.[74] If this had happened on the outward journey, it surely would not have made sense for them to continue on mass; it would have seemed politic for them to have sent a couple of members on to explain the delay and collect the notes and decisions from the chapter for distribution to the others.

## Other Journeys

As abbot, Aelred was responsible for checking on the granges and estates but, given the demands on his time and the number of holdings that Rievaulx had, it seems unlikely that Aelred visited each of them every year. Making sure that the abbey and its assets ran smoothly fell to the rest of Aelred's management team. However, given the type of man that he was, it is more than likely that Aelred, when travelling, visited any grange or estate on or near to his route.

He is also likely to have made trips to various abbeys in the Yorkshire area including Malton, Kirkham, Newburgh, Byland, Fountains and Guisborough. The other journeys he undertook included visits to York, Durham, Carlisle, Hexham, Kirkstead, Watton and London. For example, in March 1155, the relics of the saints Eata, Acca, Frethbert, Alchmund and Tilbert were moved to a new tomb within Hexham church. Aelred attended this ceremony and gave a sermon based on his *Hexham Saints* treatise.[75] The

---

[74] Ibid., 64 (from an account by Reginald of Durham).
[75] Aelred: Hexham Saints.

translation of the *Hexham Saints* is very skilful and Aelred's words flow easily as he outlines the various miracles that had taken place in and around Hexham due to devotion and faith in its saints. These miracles include examples from within his own lifetime including how Edric, one of the first Augustinian Canons, healed a woman of blindness by dipping one of Acca's bones in water and then touching her eyes with the water.

The longest journey he undertook in his lifetime was, before he became abbot, when he was sent to Rome. A journey of over one thousand miles and that was not including the three hundred plus miles from Rievaulx to Dover. We know from Bernard of Clairvaux's *Life of Malachy* one possible route: Sailing from Dover to near Wissant (quite close to Calais); then back on land via Arras, Rheims, Châlons sur Marne, Bar sur Aube, Lausanne, Martigny, and over the Great St. Bernard to Ivrea continuing on to via Vercelli, Pavia, Piacenza, Pontremoli, Lucca and Viterbo to Rome.[76] One of Malachy's trips from Ireland to Rome coincided with Aelred's mission to Rome and it is possible that they met on route.

---

[76] Bernard of Clairvaux, 1920, 74.

# Chapter 6

# No Abbey is an Island

Rievaulx abbey, like any other abbey, could not exist in isolation from the rest of society. For an abbey to survive and grow it needed income. To generate income, it needed land. To acquire land, it needed benefactors. Rievaulx had to be self-sufficient and the only way of providing resources and food for its community was by owning, and using, land. Taken together, the Abbey's holdings provided the community with most of their needs: food, heat, wool, parchment, horses, oxen, fisheries, iron, stone, and timber.[1] Benefactors, and their grants, were crucial for the survival of Rievaulx.

As abbot, it was Aelred's responsibility to ensure that Rievaulx had sufficient means to sustain itself. Aelred had to be, and was, economically and politically aware and Rievaulx thrived under his abbacy becoming the most influential Cistercian house in England in the twelfth century. The size and success of Rievaulx precluded Aelred

---

[1] Fergusson & Harrison, 42.

from being an abbot whose role was primarily one of spiritual director. Instead, he had to fit spiritual direction of the community, and his own meditation and prayer, around Rievaulx's business and political activities and needs. Dealing with benefactors, members of the secular church and politicians was a fact of life and Aelred understood that it was important to make time for them and to treat them with respect. When Walter Daniel was irritated by Aelred's time being taken up in this way, Aelred reminded him that "we expect benefits from them or we fear enmity" and therefore the time is well spent.[2]

# Benefactors

Donations were given by lords, knights and anyone with means, and included arable land, pasture land, forests (or access to them), land rich in iron ore, mills, inland waters for setting up fisheries, and, very importantly, rights of way.

## Rievaulx's Patron

The founding patron was the most important layperson associated with the abbey. The patron and his family acted as benefactors, protectors and defenders. Rievaulx's founder, Walter Espec, came from a Norman family who settled in Bedfordshire. During his lifetime, Walter acquired three lordships:

- Old Warden in Bedfordshire which he inherited from his uncle,
- Wark in Northumberland, granted to him by King Henry I, and

---

[2] Aelred: Spiritual Friendship, 69.

- Helmsley in North Yorkshire, also granted to him by King Henry I.

Walter's main residence, when not in attendance at the royal court, was Helmsley and his favourite abbey, where he eventually chose to die, was Rievaulx. As Helmsley castle was only a couple of miles away from Rievaulx, Walter was a frequent visitor. As patron he was interested in helping Rievaulx in any way he could and appreciated the counsel he received from, firstly, Abbot William, and then, later, Aelred.

The grant Rievaulx initially received from Walter included the site for the abbey buildings and nine carucates of land nearby with "all the rights of pasture, collecting dead wood and timber, water and meadow, and freedom from any secular services".[3] There was also shared use of the forest in Bilsdale, an arrangement that could only work well if there was a very good relationship between the founder and the abbey. To protect the rights of the abbey, grants were often confirmed in other ways and Rievaulx's early grants were confirmed by King Henry I in 1133 and reconfirmed in 1136 by King Stephen.

Aelred had met Walter Espec whilst still in Scotland and will have seen him on many occasions during his early years at Rievaulx. Abbot William's relationship with Walter had been a positive, easy one, and this continued under Aelred's abbacy. Rievaulx's close relationship with Walter Espec as the founder and patron will have made things much easier to manage. Unfortunately, when Walter died in about 1153 he had no direct heirs and his estates were divided between his sister's sons. Patronage of Rievaulx was inherited by the Ros

---

[3] Jamroziak, 35.

family, into which Walter's sister had married, and the relationship changed. Robert I de Ros became Walter Espec's successor as patron. He confirmed the grants that Rievaulx had received from his uncle but there is no evidence of a close relationship.[4] When Robert died in around 1162 his role was taken over by his son, Everard II. Everard confirmed Rievaulx's grants and, later, did donate some additional land to the Abbey.[5] He will have met with Aelred at various times but as he was not local to the area, it can be assumed that the relationship was not especially close.

## Other Benefactors

Aelred met a large number of influential people via his relationships with benefactors and each new contact was a possible lead for a future donation.

Attracting and keeping benefactors happy was essential for Rievaulx's survival. Whilst Aelred could not possibly be involved in all the transactions, it seems certain that the more influential, or important the donor, the more likely they would have been to expect some direct input from the abbot. Aelred will not have been able to avoid these contacts. In fact, the prosperity of Rievaulx during his reign as abbot would indicate that Aelred was very involved with, and successful at, these types of negotiations.

Over the years, Rievaulx was to receive many grants of land from various people. In Aelred's time, these included:

- A grant, in 1152, by Henry de Willardby of "5 acres in Willerby by the way to Foxholes, 2½ acres below Galeclint tending towards the bounds of Fordon and

---

4 Ibid., 45.
5 Ibid., 45.

2 ½ acres below Crostdic, also ½ acre in Greindeslac west of Midelberg for a sheepfold and a messuage at Kornedale for a dwelling for the monks and their household, also pasture for 300 sheep".[6]

- From Hugh de Malebisse, pasture and meadow in Scawton between 1154 and 1160.[7]
- From Odo de Boltby, 1142-45, land below Hesketh bordering with Boltby, Ravensthorpe and Thirlby, about ten miles west of Rievaulx.[8]
- A grant in the 1160s from Bernard de Balliol to the monks of Rievaulx "for the health of the soul of Henry II and Agnes the donor's wife and for the soul of Joscelin his uncle, of pasture for 60 brood mare in his forest of Teesdale, 6 score beasts, 12 cows, 2 bulls in Egglehope and Hudeshope by bounds within Middleton in Teesdale…"[9]
- A grant of one carucate in Marton (Grange) with a tillage from Robert de Laceles.[10] Another carucate in Reighton from Ralph de Nevill.[11]
- From Benedict, son of Gervase de Wombleton, 1145-47, land in Wombleton, Spelcross, Skiplam, Rook Borugh and Muscoates.[12]

Other important benefactors at the time included Roger de Mowbray and his mother Gundreda, both influential individuals in the Yorkshire area. Roger de Mowbray had taken part in the Second Crusade of 1147 and will have

---

6 Farrar, Vol. II, 499.
7 Farrar, Vol. III, 441
8 Jamroziak, 37, 178.
9 Farrar, Vol. I, 440.
10 Farrar, Vol. II, 70.
11 Ibid., 485.
12 Jamroziak, 37, 178.

provided first hand information to Aelred on what he had experienced and witnessed. One example of a grant from Roger de Mowbray was his grant of the vill of Welburn in around 1155. This was the first documented case of a grant of land with its serfs to a Cistercian house in England and, theoretically, a type of gift forbidden by the Cistercian rule.[13] Although Roger de Mowbray granted a whole vill with its people he also included a clause stating that the serfs might stay or leave as they wished: "Let it be known that I give all my serfs in Welburn to the Abbot of Rievaulx, without restrictions. I permit to them all freedom and to go or stay whichever they want and to whatever place they want."[14]

So, the serfs could go but if they stayed they could expect the abbey's protection and payment for their labour. It does seem a strange agreement for Rievaulx to have entered into. We can only assume that the land was of particular significance to the abbey or perhaps the serfs were a welcome asset as land could only generate income if there was enough labour to work it. It is the case that the economics, and politics, of an area will have always played a part in the type and nature of grants abbeys received and Rievaulx, like other abbeys, at times, will have bent the rules.

Sometimes the land donation received was too small to be worked on its own and so, to enable development, adjoining parcels of land were often purchased. For example, Walter Ingram granted and sold land in Welbury and Arncliffe to Rievaulx. The monks gave him 15 marks, a gold ring to Holdeard, his wife, and 2 shillings to both their sons.[15]

Another example from Aelred's time that illustrates deviation from the rule was in around 1162 when Hugh de

---

13 Ibid., 71.
14 Ibid., 72.
15 Farrar, Vol. II, 56.

Malebisse gave Rievaulx a meadow in Scawton and permission to use pasturelands. He received twenty shillings compensation from the abbey in a special ceremony in the abbey church that was witnessed by many.[16] This was, for the time, an unusual occurrence in Cistercian abbeys but reflects the way the abbey had to focus on economic interests to be able to prosper. Hugh de Malebisse was not content with just being a silent benefactor known only to the monks (and God), he wanted his gift to be publicly acknowledged. If Rievaulx wanted the land being offered Aelred had to be flexible in the terms of the donation.

Charters were drawn up to confirm donations and some form of witnessing ceremony usually took place. Some of the witnesses to these charters were frequently abbots and priors of nearby abbeys; in Rievaulx's case these included the abbots of Byland and Fountains, and priors and canons of Bridlington, Kirkham and Newburgh. Aelred will have also acted as a witness to charters for other abbeys. Witnessing of charters helped to establish and sustain friendly relationships between monastic houses and their neighbours, both lay and religious.[17]

A diverse range of donations was essential if Rievaulx's goal of self-sufficiency was to be realized. For example, salt was an essential commodity—it formed part of the Cistercian diet, was used for preserving food, tanning leather, cheese production and in the soldering of pipes and guttering.[18] Salt was obtained from water sources including seawater, springs and ground water. If an abbey had no direct access to salt they would have to purchase it and salt was expensive. It is possible that Rievaulx had access to its

---

[16] Jamroziak, 74.
[17] Ibid., 139.
[18] Williams, D. H., 375.

own source with land donations along the River Tees but we don't know if that was the case in Aelred's time. Byland, Rievaulx's neighbour, had a coastal saltpan at Coatham on the River Tees[19] and could possibly have been Rievaulx's main supplier.

The donations included land that could be used to develop iron making. Adam de Birkin granted a place to build forges on the River Dove in Stainbrough and nearby for the development of forges guaranteeing Rievaulx a monopoly of iron working in the area,[20] and forges were constructed by 1150.[21] Matthew son of Saxe gave four acres and one half perch of land in Blacker to make smithies for the manufacture of iron and utensils using iron ore and dead wood from his part of Flocton and Shitlington, near Huddersfield.[22]

## Disputes with Benefactors

Whilst benefactors were one of the Rievaulx's most valuable assets they could also become liabilities if disputes arose, and if their land was adjacent to that of the abbey, they also had the potential of becoming quarrelsome neighbours. The Cistercians tried very hard with the wording of grants and charters to minimise problems but not all problems could be avoided. As a major landowner an abbey had a massive impact on its neighbours. It was, therefore, not unusual for grants to contain phrases protecting local people's rights as in the example, given above, of Roger de Mowbray's grant.

During the late 1160s, there were a number of disputes about land with some noblemen trying to reclaim some of

---

[19] Ibid., 380.
[20] Farrar, Vol. III, 361.
[21] Burton, 263.
[22] Farrar, Vol. III, 379.

Rievaulx's lands.[23] These were not unique to Rievaulx. As the original patrons and benefactors died the number of disputes increased—heirs sometimes felt they had been short changed or simply didn't share the spiritual link of their ancestors to the abbey concerned. It would have been seen as morally wrong to attempt to take back a complete bequest so the focus of disputes was often on smaller parcels of land or issues over usage.

Disputes also arose when landowners felt that the abbey was in some way being unfair in either its land usage, for example in the case of shared pasture, or in terms of the rights of its immediate neighbours. Gilbert de Gant was an important benefactor of Rievaulx and the founder of Rievaulx's daughter house at Rufford. Soon after its foundation, Rufford experienced problems with one of Gilbert's tenants who claimed ownership of some of the land donated to the abbey and "generally harassed the monks".[24]

# Granges

As small pockets of land in isolation from each other were of little use, it made economic sense for abbeys to acquire adjoining lands. When the parcel of land was of a sufficient size a grange or estate was developed.

Early Cistercian legislation required that granges were no more than a day's ride from the abbey so that the community could keep them under adequate control.[25] The reality was somewhat different. Abbeys often received small grants of land a distance from the abbey and extended them to develop a grange or estate so that the land could be properly

---

23 Jamroziak, 47.
24 Ibid., 83.
25 Coppack, 111.

managed and worked more effectively. Rievaulx received grants that extended as far north as Middleton in Teesdale, as far south as Worsborough and, east to Scarborough. Some of the estates during Aelred's time included Low Bolton, Cowton, Griff, Skiplam, Welburn, Hesketh, Rock Barugh, Humanby, Crosby, Murton and Hawnby.[26] Some of these, including Griff and Hawnby, were within easy walking distance of Rievaulx with Griff being less than twenty minutes away, others were a few days ride away.

The granges varied enormously in size with some being little more than sheep runs whilst others were the size of small monasteries.[27] Each grange was made up of a number of farm buildings including barns and stables, an oratory and living accommodation, surrounded by a precinct wall or bank. A number of lay brothers lived on each grange under the command of a grange master who was also a lay brother.[28]

## Lay Brothers

The lay brothers were an essential element of the Cistercian Order. Without them it would have been impossible to develop granges at some distance from the abbey especially as the Cistercians were against having servants or hired hands. So, the decision was made to receive "bearded lay brothers with the permission of their bishop, and to treat them in life and in death as themselves, except for the monastic state."[29]

The lay brothers had a short beard while the monks were clean-shaven or tonsured, and the habit of the lay brothers

---

26 Fergusson & Harrison, 40.
27 Williams, D. H., 277
28 De Waal, 25.
29 De Waal, 34–5, quoting from Matarasso's Cistercian World.

was different and more adaptable to the type of work they were carrying out.[30] Becoming a lay brother, guaranteed a man a place to live and food to eat. They had to attend religious services but not as many as the monks. At a time when there was instability in the country, and work was hard to come by, the option of joining the Cistercians must have been, for many, a welcome one. We don't know how much contact with the outside world these lay brothers had as very little information about them, apart from the work they did, has survived. We do know that the larger granges had some accommodation available for guests.[31]

The number of lay brothers rapidly grew within all Cistercian abbeys. For many men it provided a way of life they could not aspire to in the secular world. As lay brothers, all their basic needs were met and, at the same time, they were working for their own salvation. Some have said it was simply a form of economic repression but I do not believe that was the intention or motivation of the Cistercians. The involvement, albeit minimal, of lay brothers in services meant that, for the first time, peasantry had access to a form of monastic life. It should also not be forgotten that manual work was not denigrated by the Cistercians but seen as spiritually important.

Without the lay brothers, and hired help, Rievaulx would not have been able to expand and grow as, quite simply, there were not enough hours in the day for the monks to carry out their religious observances and do all the work.

---

[30] Ibid., 35.
[31] Williams, D. H., 281.

# Relationships with other Abbeys

The development and expansion of monastic houses in twelfth century England was rapid and unforeseen. Men and women flooded to join the new foundations. Patrons and benefactors were easy to find and the relationships between the various houses, whether Cistercian, Augustinian, Premonstratensian or Gilbertine, were quite informal and relaxed relying on the relationships between abbots and priors and their strong religious and spiritual convictions.

As the heady days of the "new start" began to wane, the practical, economic, issues had to be addressed and dealt with in more formal ways. For example, 1164 saw the signing of an agreement between the Cistercian and Gilbertine Orders. Some of the issues addressed included:

- setting the distance between their respective granges,
- agreeing not to accept canons, monks or novices from each other, and
- agreeing not to hire servants who had not fulfilled their contracts with the other order.[32]

The witnesses to this agreement reflect the Yorkshire and Lincolnshire location of the Cistercians and the Gilbertines: they included Aelred, Abbot Geoffrey of Clairvaux, Richard of Fountains, Walter of Kirkstead, Ralph of Louth Park, Gilbert of Sempringham, Adam of Lincoln, Richard of Lindley, Thomas de Ormesby, Ralph of Watton, and Robert of Malton.

---

[32] Jamroziak, 159.

## Nearest Neighbours

As Monastic establishments grew in number and size, competition for land donations increased and, as the twelfth century moved on, problems began to arise. There was little land left that could be donated, many of the original benefactors had died and their heirs contested donations.

Abbeys, priories and monasteries of different orders found themselves with packages of land near to each other and had to find a way to coexist peacefully. Rievaulx's monastic neighbours included:

- Cistercians at Byland, Fountains, and Jervaulx.
- Augustinians at Kirkham, Newburgh, Bridlington and Guisborough.
- Gilbertines at Malton.
- Premonstratensians at Easby.
- Benedictines at York and Whitby.

The type of relationship between the abbeys and priories varied greatly. There will have been fraternal links with other Cistercian houses and more formal relationships with those of other orders. As the Cistercians were little involved in "good works", links with other orders could provide a channel for charitable giving. For example, we know that Aelred arranged that the hospital at Spital Bridge, founded by an earlier abbot of Whitby, received annually the old clothes of the Rievaulx community and that these were always sent on the feast of St Martin.[33]

Many of the monastic houses shared benefactors and patrons. For example, Walter Espec, Rievaulx's patron, was also the founder of Kirkham Priory, and Roger de Mowbray

---

[33] Young, 364.

was benefactor of Rievaulx, Byland and Newburgh. Not only were abbeys in any single area competitors for grants from the same pool of benefactors, they often had estates adjoining each other with some shared usage rights. During Aelred's abbacy the Cistercian General Chapter adopted a number of regulations to help reduce problems between neighbouring Cistercian abbeys. These included setting the minimum distance between the granges of two abbeys to at least five miles, and not allowing the development of new abbeys to be any nearer than twenty five miles to existing ones.

They also had in place a system for dealing with problems. If there was a dispute between two Cistercian abbots, then a neighbouring Cistercian abbot would be asked to arbitrate and if this failed then the issue could be taken to the General Chapter. The abbots of Rievaulx were often instructed by the General Chapter to mediate in disputes.[34] For example, Aelred was asked to mediate between the Abbey of Savigny in Normandy and, its daughter house, Furness in Cumbria in their dispute over the control of Byland Abbey.

Rievaulx's nearest neighbour was Byland, a Savignac foundation until 1147 when the Savignac order became part of the Cistercians. Co-operation between the two abbeys was essential as, not only did they have to coexist in close proximity, they shared at least one prominent benefactor in Roger de Mowbray.

Byland had experienced many difficulties in finding a permanent home and the site they were given in 1142 caused conflict with Rievaulx. The nearness of the abbeys to each other caused confusion and disruption with the monks being

---

[34] Jamroziak, 136.

unsure whether the bell they could hear, signifying a change in activity, was in fact theirs or belonged to the other abbey. This was not simply a question of not having clocks to synchronise the bells but one of different timetables as, at that point, Byland was still a Savignac house and had a different schedule to Rievaulx.

When Byland relocated to a new site, the bells ceased being an issue but difficulties still existed between the two abbeys. Their proximity inevitably meant that some of their donated lands were very near to each other. Trespass and damage, by man and animal, were the main issues followed by access to certain routes and water. On the information that we have, mainly from the Rievaulx Cartulary, it seems that during Aelred's time the relationship between the two abbeys was harmonious.[35] Rievaulx and Byland were fortunate in both having abbots in office for many years: Roger had been abbot of Byland before it became a Cistercian house and he outlived Aelred who was Rievaulx's abbot for twenty years.

Around 1165, the abbots of Clairvaux and Cîteaux expressed their concern about preserving "brotherly peace and love" between Byland and Rievaulx.[36] At this point in history we are only a couple of years away from Aelred's death and his ill health will have minimised his involvement in some of the more mundane secular issues the abbey had to deal with. Whatever the issues were we know that Roger and Aelred remained friends and that Roger anointed Aelred when he was dying and kept vigil, with other abbots, during his last days.[37]

---

[35] Ibid., 136
[36] Ibid., 145
[37] Daniel, 59, 60–61.

There is a charter in place a few years after Aelred's death which outlines in detail the boundaries and rights of the two abbeys in respect of each other. It also contains a dispute resolution process which includes punishment of any monk caught trespassing by flogging in the chapter house.[38] It is interesting that no such charter was necessary during Aelred's time as abbot and I doubt that Aelred would have agreed with the punishment aspect of the dispute process. He appears always to have gone out of his way to seek a peaceful solution.

# Templars

One other Order that was acquiring land in the Yorkshire and Lincolnshire areas at this time was the Templars and they will have shared some of the same benefactors as Rievaulx as is the case, once again, with Roger de Mowbray.

We rather strangely know nothing about Rievaulx's relationship with the Templars yet there were strong links between the two orders. The founder Hugh de Payens was a Burgundinian Lord who was probably related to Bernard of Clairvaux.[39] Another member of the original group of nine was André of Montand, an uncle of Bernard's.[40] In 1128 a council took place at Troyes during which the Templars were recognised as an official religious order. The Rule that the Templars adopted and that was ratified at this conference is believed to have been written by Bernard.[41]

Bernard was certainly in full support of the order, praising them as ideal Christian soldiers. His views on the

---

[38] Jamroziak, 141
[39] Seward, 22.
[40] Armstrong, 208.
[41] Sewrad, 22.

Templars can be read in his tract *In Praise of the New Knighthood* probably written shortly after the Troyes Council.[42] The knights, in Bernard's view, were perfect in every way, and, in contrast to worldly knights, they were assured eternal salvation.[43] The similarities of the Templars Rule to that of the Cistercians has led to them being seen, by some, as the military arm of the Cistercians but whilst there was a close relationship and some similarities, the two orders were separate and different in many significant ways.

Differences and similarities aside, the reality is that the Yorkshire Cistercians must have had relationships with the Templars but no details of these have remained. We do know that during King Stephen's reign there were about sixty charters, royal and private, issued in favour of the English Templars as these were preserved in later transcripts.[44] It was also during this time period that saw the beginning of "their great influence in Lincolnshire and the North".[45] Not long before his death, King Stephen issued a general charter to the Templars confirming their liberties and all the gifts received to that time. It is a charter that is confirmed by his successor, King Henry II.[46]

Lees identifies Richard of Hastings as the Master of the Templars in England from January 1155. In the same month Richard is recorded as having quitclaimed land in Lincolnshire to the monks of Kirkstead, a Cistercian abbey near to Revesby. This coincides with Henry II's first visit to Lincolnshire after his coronation. Later in 1155, Richard is recorded as witnessing a royal charter issued to Rievaulx

---

[42] Bernard of Clairvaux, 2000.
[43] Bulst-Thiele, 60.
[44] Lees, xli.
[45] Ibid., xli.
[46] Ibid., xlvii.

Abbey at Westminster.[47] In 1161 he is once again witness to an exchange between the Lincolnshire Templars and the monks of Kirkstead Abbey.[48] It is impossible that some links between Rievaulx and the Templars didn't exist.

There is a slim possibility that the Templars land never adjoined any of Rievaulx's but it is an unlikely scenario. The more realistic option is that the details of these relationships were, at some point, removed from the record, probably after the Order of the Knights Templar was disbanded.

# Bishops and Archbishops

The Cistercian Order was independent of the diocesan structure and bishops did not have power over the abbeys but the Cistercians were still part of the church. It was also the case that, whilst the Cistercian Order was outside of the mainstream structure, it still wanted to influence it.

The Cistercians not only needed to be involved in order to protect their economic assets but also to exert influence on the way things were done. In the early days, under the influence of Bernard of Clairvaux, the Cistercians saw part of their mission as campaigning against corruption within the church, and influencing secular clergy in their spiritual worldview. Aelred preached at clerical synods and councils and was concerned with encouraging the highest standards of conduct for clergy.

Two key political figures in the country's church hierarchy were the Archbishop of York and the Bishop of Durham.

---

[47] Ibid., xlix.
[48] Ibid., liii.

# York

Rievaulx, and the majority of its estates, were located in the diocese of York and the archbishop of York played a significant role in Rievaulx's history. Archbishop Thurstan, known to Aelred since boyhood, was involved in the early negotiations regarding Rievaulx's foundation and in its establishment. He will have visited the site and had many discussions with Walter Espec and the Cistercian monks regarding the site and the abbey's foundation.

After Thurstan died, the Cistercians, including Rievaulx, tried to influence the election of the next Archbishop believing firmly that their views were the correct ones and that they had every right to try reform the mainstream church. They were not successful until the election, in 1146, of a Cistercian Pope who ensured that Henry Murdac, Cistercian abbot of Fountains, was chosen as archbishop of York.

Cistercian relationships with York archbishops were not always smooth. Roger de Pont L'Évêque was appointed in 1154 and he was particularly keen to reform and expand the church. To do this he needed resources which led to conflict with some Cistercian houses. The Cistercians had, somewhat contentiously, been exempt from paying tithes and this had reduced the church's income—disputes and antagonism were not uncommon but it appears that Archbishop Roger had a positive relationship with Aelred. This may have been helped by the fact that Rievaulx seemed to have gone out of its way not to acquire property with tithes so the issue of non-payment of them rarely arose. Nonetheless, during Aelred's time, Archbishop Roger issued charters of protection to Rievaulx Abbey but not to Fountains.[49] These types of

---

[49] Jamroziak, 178.

charter confirmations will have taken place in York and Aelred, as Rievaulx's abbot, will have been present.

## Durham

During Aelred's time there was a great deal of contact with the bishops of Durham, and Aelred's strong family connections with the Durham area will have been an important factor in the harmonious nature of these contacts.

Around 1150, he was part of a group of abbots and priors, including the abbot of Newminster and the prior of Tynemouth, who were asked to intervene in a conflict about seniority between Prior Roger and Archdeacon Wazo of Durham.[50] As Aelred's name opens the charter that outlines their findings and decision, it seems that he had been allocated the role of "chairman".

In 1152, Rievaulx received a grant of land in Crosby from William of St Barbe, the bishop of Durham. This was more than a land donation as it came with a promise of support and protection for the abbey.[51] These were about to be vital for Rievaulx as Walter Espec, the abbey's patron was now ageing and had retired to be a monk at the abbey. Aelred will have always sought ways to protect Rievaulx and will have been aware that Rievaulx's situation would change when Walter died. In return for his grant the bishop received prayers for his soul. Unfortunately, the bishop died towards the end of 1152. His successor was Hugh du Puiset but his election was challenged by Henry Murdac, the archbishop of York at the time, and quite an acrimonious situation raged on until May 1154.[52] There is little information on the links

---

[50] Offler, 147–8.
[51] Jamroziak, 185.
[52] Scammell, 1956.

with Rievaulx from this point but it can, I think reasonably be assumed, that some form of support continued.

## Lincoln

Aelred will also have had contacts with the bishop of Lincoln over the years as two of Rievaulx's daughter houses, Revesby and Rufford, were in the Lincoln diocese. We also know that when he was at Revesby the bishop of Lincoln, at the time, invited Aelred to preach at local church councils and to assist in the reform of the clergy.[53]

# Aelred's Style and Approach

As Rievaulx prospered under Aelred, we know he was very successful in his role as "Chief Executive Officer". The men who served in his management team must have been inspired by his example as it does seem that during Aelred's abbacy there were very few disputes. Aelred was obviously well respected both inside and outside Rievaulx. I suspect his mission statement would have run along the lines of:

> Rievaulx abbey is a Cistercian abbey providing safety and security to all who enter it in their quest to find union with God.

> In the way that God welcomes all to his kingdom, Rievaulx welcomes all men to its community.

> We will strive to meet all the needs of our community by our own toil. We understand that to achieve this we are dependent on the goodwill of others. We will at all times cherish the generosity of our patron and benefactors and treat them with

---

[53] Daniel, 28.

> love and respect, remembering that it is their kindness that enables Rievaulx to exist.
>
> At all times, we will strive to remember in our thoughts, prayers and actions that all men are our brothers in Christ.

Aelred embraced benefactors in the same way he embraced anyone who wished to join the community at Rievaulx—with open arms. If their grants came with unusual or not generally accepted conditions then so be it. As long as Rievaulx gained, and was in no way compromised, then any grant was welcome. Wherever possible he followed the regulations of the Cistercian General Chapter but he did not adhere to any if the end result meant alienation of a benefactor or a loss for Rievaulx.

Did Aelred resent his role in worldly affairs? I don't think so. He had a great example to follow in the way William, Rievaulx's first abbot, had run Rievaulx. He will also have discussed concerns with other abbots and, maybe even directly with Bernard of Clairvaux. I suspect his solution to dealing with duties that were not overtly spiritual was to convert them into a spiritual activity. In the way that Zen Buddhism teaches that any and all activity is, or can be, a meditation practice, I think Aelred saw his non-spiritual activities as a way of practising the Cistercian principles of love and charity. He saw his role as abbot as one given to him by God and hence every aspect of the role needed to be embraced with the same love and fervour as time spent in actual prayer and contemplation.

His approach to political affairs will have been the same. It has been suggested that, like Saint Bernard, Aelred was drawn into the affairs of Church and kingdom, but was more successful than Bernard in avoiding entanglement, that he was in some way less inclined to these involvements.[54] Looking at Aelred's activities over the years, I think his involvement in politics was quite extensive but that he saw his primary role as securing Rievaulx's future and wherever possible promoting and fostering the Cistercian way, and peace in his country.

He was drawn into the affairs of the state but avoided entanglement. Whereas Bernard preached for the crusade and was keen to destroy Abelard, Aelred maintained his silence and always sought for reconciliation. It was as if he saw in all those he met the touch of God and was unable to condemn, seeking always to understand and to help. We know he had contact and influence with various kings, archbishops and bishops. His opinion was sought after and his reputation for compassion was widespread. Walter Daniel tells us that Aelred sent letters to:

> "the lord Pope, to the King of France, the King of England, the King of Scotland, the Archbishops of Canterbury and York and nearly every bishop in England".[55]

Aelred was able to embrace all men he came into contact with, and the inner peace he had achieved radiated out from him to touch all who came into contact with him. He did not see himself as a man of influence but as man through whom God worked. The loss of his correspondence prevents us from knowing the extent of his social and political influence but it certainly seems to be the case that, first and foremost, he saw himself as an abbot and spiritual educator.

---

[54] Aelred: Mirror of Charity; Dumont, introduction, 40.
[55] Daniel, 42.

# Chapter 7

# Spiritual Director and Writer

As abbot, Aelred was head of the monastic community at Rievaulx. He occupied the first place in the church, chanted the solemn mass on major festivals, and blessed the candles, ashes, palms and paschal fire. He received novices, heard confessions, presided at the daily chapter, and gave holy water to the monks at Compline. As abbot, he occupied the place of Christ in the monastery,[1] and was a person to whom "the utmost respect and obedience were due".[2]

Aelred influenced every aspect of the monastery's routines and daily activities. His personality, compassion and love of God permeated out from him to all the members of the community, monks and lay brothers alike. He was

---

[1] Benedict, 11.
[2] Williams, D. H., 71.

sometimes called "Bernard of the North" because "he did for Rievaulx, vocation-wise, what Bernard had achieved at Clairvaux".[3] The community at Rievaulx became so large under Aelred's rule that on feast days the church was crowded with community members "like bees in a hive" unable to move in any direction because of the numbers.[4] In 1132 Rievaulx had a community of about twenty-five, by 1142 it had risen to around three hundred and, by 1165, to six hundred and fifty, about two thirds of whom were lay brothers.[5]

As abbot, Aelred was expected to teach by his words and deeds according to the needs of his monks: he had to adapt and fit himself to all and ensure that he did not lose any of the flock entrusted to him.[6] Aelred took the role very seriously and embraced it in a way that most abbots never could. He adopted the Cistercian ideal of equality as fully as is possible by ensuring that Rievaulx was open to *all* men.

The egalitarian aspect of monastic life extended beyond status to the non-ownership of goods and attachments to work roles. Aelred acknowledged the differences between individual monks in respect of their talents, their physical strength, infirmities and personalities. He advocated neither pride nor humility; rather an understanding that all an individual has is by the grace of God and is for him to use to benefit all, hence what belongs to one belongs to all. The monastic community flourished on this sharing and understanding of each individual's worth whether they were a monk or a lay brother.

---

[3] Williams, D. H., 64.
[4] Daniel, 38.
[5] Knowles, 258–9.
[6] Benedict, 13.

Daniel tells us that Aelred believed that all, whether weak or strong, should find peace and love at Rievaulx.[7] During his abbacy, Rievaulx was closed only to women. Men flocked from "the far ends of the earth" and many who could not gain entrance to other monastic houses arrived at Rievaulx and were admitted.[8] During the seventeen years Walter Daniels spent under Aelred's abbacy he never saw him expel a single monk: "Four, it is true, left him without his knowledge, but the Lord led them all back save one".[9]

Aelred saw the Cistercian life as one open to all men and not restricted to the few. To truly follow in Jesus' footsteps, everyone had to be welcome and everyone was but this was not commonplace. Usually some restrictions or a selection procedure were in place to protect the monastic community. Aelred's approach was different, special in its own way, and a testament to both his faith and the solidity of his vocation. There will have been many who saw it as wrong as unstable elements could cause disharmony but, during Aelred's abbacy, Rievaulx maintained its open door policy and the critics were treated as gently and with the same degree of patience as anyone else.

## The Monastic Experience

Aelred understood that the journey of the individual soul back to God was not an easy one and that being part of a community could help the individual. The support of living and working with others following the same path could make the individual's journey easier.

---

[7] Daniel, 37.
[8] Ibid., 37.
[9] Ibid., 40.

The monk, by leaving secular society, freed himself from the demands and expectations of family and society, was able to avoid many temptations, and commit himself to a single goal—that of finding God. He did this with the support of his fellow monks. He donned a robe, owned nothing, followed orders and submitted to a Rule. He committed himself to understanding, and not running away from, himself. The whole process potentially made men very vulnerable and without the support and understanding of fellow monks could, and sometimes did, lead to mental instability.

Living with others always presents challenges; living in a closed monastic community presents even more challenges. There is nowhere for the monks to hide from their feelings and they soon discover that loving everyone is not always easy. The smallest things have the ability to turn into enormous issues: a sense of righteous indignation bubbling to the surface at another monk's apparent laziness or snobbery, the novelty of not having to make any decisions being replaced by feelings of irritation and a sense of unfairness.

These feelings are in fact essential to the whole experience as they enable the individual monk to face his inner demons and move beyond them. Rationalising and thinking would only take a monk so far. At some point there has to be an emotional change; a point at which the monk lets go of all that is "self" and allows God fully in. There is no doubt in my mind that Aelred managed to do this. He is described as being patient, always having time for others, of being a good listener, and being able to settle disputes easily. Aelred certainly had the ability to relate well with men from all walks of life. His relationships with benefactors and church officials seem a great deal less fraught than some of those of his contemporaries. He was prepared to accept anyone into Rievaulx and to work with them; guiding them along the path, which, despite living in a community, was something that had to be done alone—internally.

The path of freeing one's soul to find union with God is not always a comfortable or easy one. Aelred seemed to have a true grasp of the path and all of its hurdles. He understood that all could follow the path but that the actual route would be different for each individual monk. The insecurities, fears and thoughts of each individual would vary; where some would stumble, others would pass easily. His role as a spiritual director was to, gently, guide each monk along the path by helping them reach an understanding from their own side rather than by simply being told to follow a set of rules. The rules and regulations existed because they assisted in the process of freeing the soul so that it could embark on its journey to God but the following of the rules alone would not suffice.

## Aelred's Style and Approach

The monks were a diverse bunch: there were intellectuals with their subtle perplexities and doubts, men who could not read or write, sinners who had come to break away from their old habits, individuals who were already very saintly; some were used to an easy life with many comforts whilst others had lived very hard lives in poverty.[10]

Aelred had an amazing amount of patience with his monks and that, with Rievaulx's open door policy, tell us a great deal about his fundamental beliefs. He understood, as well as believed, that the image of God resided in *all*, not just

---

[10] Merton, IV, 51.

those judged to be good or worthy, and because that was the case, everyone was capable of finding true union with God. "There was no one wild enough, wicked enough, violent enough, ungrateful enough to be beyond the range of Aelred's forgiveness and forbearance and tender mercy."[11] He knew that the problems any monk experienced arose in the mind and could only be resolved there: as Squire puts it, "whether what happens to a man brings him peace or trouble is determined simply by his state of mind".[12]

When the individual monk fully realized this, he could allow God in and everything would begin to change for him. Whilst worldly events would still take place and problems would arise, they would not disturb the mind which had found peace and rest in God's love. The monk would be able to meet life's challenges with an equanimity that led him to embrace others rather than to push them away. He would still have preferences for people and things but would not be attached to them to the exclusion of others.

As abbot, Aelred successfully created the conditions and provided the inspiration for his monks to move along this path: "in his subjects and in all who came under his spiritual influence, Aelred tried to ensure the conditions for healthy, unstultified growth."[13] Aelred fully understood the wanderings and restlessness of the mind and the body. In his *Rule of Life for a Recluse* he wrote:

> "When the psalms attract you use them, but when they become a burden change to reading; when reading palls rouse yourself to prayer; when wearied of them all take to manual labour. By this

[11] Merton, III, 75.
[12] Squire, 33.
[13] Ibid., 130.

healthy alternation you will refresh your spirit and banish spiritual weariness."[14]

Aelred understood that it did no good to talk at certain types of individuals—it only upset them to be told they were wrong. He took the wise, patient route and chose to listen to them, to be empathic, and to gently, at the right moment, guide them forward with a question or observation. He was truly skilful in his ability to embrace others and work with them so that they too could experience the inner peace of true communion with God.

Among the new recruits were educated men, thinkers and intellectuals and their need to discuss and speculate on their thoughts and ideas were, despite the rule of silence, catered for. Debate and discussion of theology were not the norm in the Cistercian order yet, at various times, we get glimpses of Aelred as part of a group of monks in discussion. After his rooms were built for him alongside the infirmary he held what can only be described as impromptu seminars: "for every day they came to it and sat in it, twenty or thirty at a time, to talk together of the spiritual delights of the Scriptures and of the observance of the Order".[15] I suspect that these seminars had also taken place prior to Aelred having his own rooms, perhaps in the refectory.

Aelred must have felt secure enough in his role as abbot to allow these discussions to take place. He recognised a need in some of his monks to talk, to discuss and share their ideas and, rather than trying to force everyone into the same mould, he responded to it. The harmony that was found within such a large community, given the diversity of people admitted, is to quote Thomas Merton "something of a

---

[14] Aelred: Rule of Life for a Recluse, 56.
[15] Daniel, 40.

modern miracle".[16] It could only have been very deep belief, conviction, and love that managed to fuse together such a disparate number of men into a thriving, cohesive and harmonious community.

In the years after Aelred's death things changed and more stringent rules were introduced so we must assume that the harmony was in great part due to Aelred's influence and personality. As Aelred was away from Rievaulx a lot of time, he must also have been able to infuse others with his belief in everyone's worth otherwise he would have always returned to face innumerable problems. To me, it appears that Aelred had truly found union with God. His soul was at peace and his love was universal in the sense that he could see the image of God in each and every individual. He never became angry because he no longer experienced anger, he did not need to defend himself against critics as he was in no way threatened. He radiated compassion to all and expressed his love openly.

"Aelred loved his monks with an affection that was altogether unique. It was something born of grace. It transcended the natural order".[17] Aelred openly wrote and spoke of his love for his monks and his words, to us, can seem strange as love in the modern world is more usually applied to the love of parents for their children or in respect of romantic relationships. Our conventions restrict our use of the word but Aelred did not live within these conventions. He radiated an energy that attracted others to it. The majority were warmed and inspired by it, some were threatened and ill at ease and lashed out against him but none could avoid its influence.

---

[16] Merton, IV, 50.
[17] Ibid., 53.

# Religious Writings

Aelred, and some other twelfth century Cistercian writers, are still read and studied today. Yet they were not writing about anything "new". What set them apart from many of their predecessors was their approach. The writings of the early Cistercians contain greater elements of personal conviction and almost mysticism: "the White Monks speak with accents of a more personal and more lyrical conviction that everywhere betrays the influence of an intimate and mystical experience".[18] The theme of all their writing is the union of the soul with God, which, by its nature, is a very personal, intimate, and mystical experience.

Aelred's religious writings differ greatly from his historical works which were aimed at a wider audience. The religious writings were intended solely for monks and this is reflected in the subject matter and the style of writing. Aelred is acutely aware that individual monks are at different stages in their inner development and he takes them gently step by step through his reasoning towards understanding. He wrote "with the serenity of the man who is sure of himself and quietly aware of the foibles and difficulties of his hearers".[19]

Aelred's enthusiasm for scripture as a source for meditation is evident throughout his religious writings. As the truth of Scripture "stems from its ultimate infallible source" those who meditate on scripture are guided to that truth. By using the scriptures directly as a source of meditation one is learning about, and following, the example of Jesus himself.[20]

---

[18] Daniel, 18.
[19] Daniel: Powicke, introduction, xxiii.
[20] Sommerfeldt, 48–9.

One of Aelred's major themes is that love of others and God is essential for an individual's happiness. Love of others must extend to all including enemies. He stresses that friendship stems from love but is not the same as love and, whilst we must love everyone, we will only chose some people as our friends. Good friends need to be loyal, trustworthy, a pleasure to be with, concerned about our well being and sensitive. Spiritual friendship is a step towards love and knowledge of God.

In loving others, we are not embracing them all into our lives. Aelred's references to "serving one's neighbour" usually means praying for them, weeping over them and so forth and not any form of active service.[21] Loving others was more about generating the feelings of love, compassion and understanding but not active service. The Cistercians did give alms to the poor and medical care but the ideal was a closed community in which the individual monk could focus on his own salvation. The idea of unity with God through service to others was not really present in Cistercian theology.

In his religious writings, Aelred uses examples from his personal life to illustrate certain points. It is tempting to jump on these examples as providing insights into Aelred's own life and many modern day writers have done just that, and, in the process, have totally ignored the actual purpose of the examples. Aelred wrote to provide help and guidance to other monks, and analysis of any aspect of his religious writings must focus on what Aelred was attempting to teach others and not what he was saying about himself.

Examples, purporting to be from his own life, are only present in the books because Aelred thought they would be a

---

21 Bynum, 71.

useful tool in getting his message over to his readers. They are not, and never were, definitive statements about Aelred the man. Perhaps one of Aelred's failings was a touch too much humility. By using examples of his own faults and problems, he was simply attempting to show the monks that he was no different from them: he too had faults and difficulties and, if he could overcome them, then so could they. Unfortunately, for Aelred's reputation, some individuals have taken these examples way too literally, coloured them with their own perceptions and prejudices, developed and then presented theories to the world that really have no basis in a reality other than the one they have constructed in their own imaginations.

Aelred was a very intelligent man and very aware of the audience he was writing for. His historical works demonstrate this very clearly as within them he shows his political astuteness and demonstrates through reason and example the point he wants to make. They are relevant to the time, politically aware and non-contentious. His religious writings are as astute. The intended readers are monks from various backgrounds and with differing degrees of understanding. Aelred wants to inspire and help them all. He understands that one way of doing this is, by showing them that others have experienced the same problems and difficulties as they are experiencing. He is not highlighting his own past weaknesses rather he is sharing a moment of *spiritual* intimacy with them and he is only able do this because he has attained a level of spirituality from which love and forgiveness are as natural to him as breathing.

It is also strange that when Aelred talks about the loss of his own virginity that some people have assumed that it was with a man and not a woman yet there is absolutely nothing in what he writes to indicate this in any way and, once again, they have missed the point. The only reason Aelred mentioned losing his virginity was because of his awareness that the greater majority of his monks had sexual relationships prior to entering the abbey: he wanted to reassure them and he did this in typical Aelred style by saying look at me, I am no different to you—I also was a sinner. He wanted them to feel okay about themselves, to understand that what they were going through was not unusual and that even their abbot had undergone those experiences and problems.

Aelred's religious writings were intended for use in the monastery and in the twelfth century. Whilst they still have some relevance today, misunderstandings can, and do, arise when they are read out of context.

## Pastoral Prayer

It is likely that Aelred wrote his *Pastoral Prayer*[22] whilst abbot of Rievaulx. Although there is no date, the content of the prayer would suggest that he had been an abbot for some time. The prayer was written for his own use and for use by others in similar roles. Squire describes the prayer as coming "nearest to being the embodiment of what his personal ideal finally came to be".[23]

The prayer is delightful. It is a direct plea from the heart of Aelred to God for guidance, forgiveness, and wisdom to enable him to carry out his role of abbot as well as possible. Aelred is acutely aware of the role he has in helping others with their spiritual life and wants to do the best he can when guiding them. He writes:

---

[22] Aelred: Pastoral Prayer.
[23] Squire, 150.

"Teach me to suit myself to everyone according to his nature, character and disposition, according to his power of understanding or his lack of it, as time and place require, in each case, as you would have me do."[24]

The prayer is gentle, open, honest, and filled with compassion for his monks. Aelred wants to do the very best for them and asks for God's guidance and blessings to be given directly to each of them as well as to himself. Its openness, vulnerability, gentleness and humility make it a joy to read.

## Jesus at the Age of Twelve

Aelred wrote *On Jesus at the Age of Twelve*[25] around 1153-57 and addressed it directly to a monk named Ivo at Warden, one of Rievaulx's daughter houses. Aelred uses the technique of addressing his writing to one individual as a method of making the teaching more direct and personal to the reader.

The treatise deals with a specific episode mentioned in Luke's Gospel (Luke 2:41-50) when Jesus, at twelve years of age, goes with his parents to Jerusalem for the festival of Passover. After the festival ended "the boy Jesus stayed behind in Jerusalem, but his parents did not know it".[26] Three days later they found him in the temple in Jerusalem "sitting among the teachers, listening to them and asking them questions".[27]

Aelred's aim is not to explain the bible passage but to show how it can be used as a meditation exercise; it is an

---

24 Aelred: Pastoral Prayer, 115.
25 Aelred: On Jesus at the Age of Twelve
26 Bible, Luke 2:43, 1243.
27 Bible: Luke 2:43, 2:46, 1243.

early example of Christian teaching that uses the life of Jesus in this way. Aelred describes his aim as follows: "I hope to be able to explain your progress to you through this passage from the Gospel, so that you may read in these pages what you are experiencing with interior joy in yourself."[28] Aelred suggests that the monks take the:

- birth of Jesus as the model of their spiritual birth, their "conversion to holiness";
- Herod's persecution as symbolic of the temptations they experience at the beginning of their conversion;
- Jesus' life in Nazareth as the next stage in their spiritual advancement, and,
- finally, Jesus' arrival in Jerusalem as the stage of contemplation of heavenly secrets.

As Squire notes, it is through works such as this one that Aelred "was able to communicate to others a sense of the possibilities of the life of prayer and of affective contact with the person of Jesus Christ."[29]

## Sermons

In his role as Abbot, of both Revesby and Rievaulx, Aelred gave many sermons. He preached within his own abbey, at Rievaulx's daughter houses and possibly other abbeys; sometimes at churches when visiting in an area and at significant gatherings outside the cloister. Walter Daniel tells us that Aelred "preached about two hundred most eloquent

---

[28] Aelred: On Jesus at the Age of Twelve, 25.
[29] Squire, 69.

sermons, worthy of all praise, in our chapters, in synods and to the people".[30]

The types of sermons Aelred gave within Rievaulx fell into two main categories. Firstly, each day, in the chapter house, immediately after the celebration of the office of Prime in church, a passage of Saint Benedict's *Rule* was read aloud and Aelred would give a sermon or commentary on it. Secondly, on "special days", Aelred preached to the whole Rievaulx community, including the lay brothers. These special days included the fifteen principal days in the church's calendar and the anniversary of the dedication of the abbey's church. Twenty-eight of these sermons have recently been translated.[31] They include sermons for the Nativity of the Lord, Easter, the Feast of St Benedict, the Feast of the Holy Apostles Peter and Paul, and for the Assumption of Saint Mary. The sermons are based on the Gospel reading used in the service on the feast day.

Aelred's sermons gave monks what they were familiar with, and what corresponded to their daily life and experience. The sermons were designed to clarify basic monastic themes, to provide comfort and hope: their teaching "rich, not pedestrian... elevated but neither abstract nor theoretical."[32]

Aelred's sermons go far beyond being simple commentaries on the gospel readings. Rather, Aelred takes the reading and explains how its message is of direct relevance to his audience of monks and lay brothers. Throughout the sermons, he outlines the stages of the path towards true union with God. He shows how the monastic community is helpful and supportive—the monks daily

---

[30] Daniel, 42.
[31] Aelred: Liturgical Sermons.
[32] Aelred: Liturgical Sermons: Basil Pennington, introduction, 32.

interactions with each other hold up a mirror to them of the traits and ideas they need to change to bring them to the state of being able to love all equally.

The sermons provide an excellent window for us into how Aelred taught and shared his understanding of Christianity and the Cistercian way of life. He skilfully uses imagery to convey his meaning. For example, one of the sermons included in the collection deals with Christmas and Aelred takes, as his starting point, the decree from Emperor Augustus that the entire world should be registered. As the "whole globe is subject to our emperor—that is, to God" all men should register themselves with God.[33] Emperors usually expect some form of payment and God is no different but what is it that he expects? "Doubtless it is our soul, which bears within itself his image".[34]

As God made man in his image, that image must reside in man's soul and man's best gift to God is to restore his image to him. Whilst alive, men are not part of God's city but live in cities of their choice. In respect of the Cistercian way of life he said: "Our way of life is a strongly fortified city surrounded on all sides by sound observances which, like walls and towers, rise up to prevent our enemy from deceiving us and enticing us away".[35]

Poverty defends the monks "against the pride of the world, against harmful and ruinous vanities and superfluities". Silence repels quarrels, dissension and detraction. Each aspect of the rule including obedience, humility, the diet and clothing all act as towers and walls of protection.[36] The community provides the individual monk

---

33 Aelred: Liturgical Sermons, 91–92.
34 Ibid., 92.
35 Ibid., 93.
36 Ibid., 93.

with protection and is to be honoured and respected. Using the shepherd analogy, Aelred describes how each monk must be the careful shepherd of his own thoughts and actions, guarding and protecting them so that his soul comes to no harm.[37]

We know that Aelred also produced a series of sermons on the burdens of Isaiah. The process began in an Advent sermon sent to Gilbert Foliot, bishop of London. Aelred was then asked by his monks to develop his observations which he does in thirty one sermons.[38] Squire tells us that the sermons were "no mean undertaking for a sick and busy man to perfect so elaborate a work, half treatise and half commentary".[39]

## Spiritual Friendship

The book *Spiritual Friendship* explores the different facets of friendship and is divided into three parts. It is written as a dialogue between Aelred and various monks. In the first part the monk is Ivo and it appears to be set in Warden. In parts two and three, the monks are Walter Daniel and Gratian and the setting is Rievaulx.

The different characters probably arise from the fact that the book was started as early as 1140 but not completed until the mid 1160s.[40] The long gap between start and completion, I suspect has more to do with the subject matter rather than a lack of time. The original idea will have been discussed with others including Abbot William and was probably discouraged. If the completion year of around 1164 is correct, I think it is indicative of Aelred approaching the end

---

[37] Ibid., 97–8.
[38] Sommerfeldt, xvii-xviii; Squire, 134–9.
[39] Squire, 135.
[40] Aelred: Spiritual Friendship; Roby, introduction, 22.

of his life and wanting to leave behind his views on a topic close to his heart. By 1164 there was no one in the Cistercian community who would advice against Aelred's decision and, as abbot, he required no ones permission.

Aelred stresses that spiritual friendship differs from other friendships and is cemented by "similarity of life, morals, and pursuits among the just... it is a mutual conformity in matters human and divine united with benevolence and charity".[41] Love, he writes, has to be developed for all especially our neighbours—for a monk this especially means his fellow monks. That one will inevitably be drawn more to some monks rather than others is a fact of life, but the choice of a spiritual friend must be done wisely and with objectivity as spiritual friendship can only arise from true love and must be tested before it is wholly entered into.

Aelred realizes, fully realizes, very early on that his spirituality can only be deepened by loving all those around him. He takes as his example Jesus who is the one friend all the monks, and all men, have in common. Aelred explores the concept of spiritual friendship from his experience as a Cistercian, his knowledge of scripture, saints' lives, his own secular life and other writers. His goal is to draw up rules for "a chaste and holy love".[42] He is not writing as an idealist but as a realist; he knows that certain types of friendship can be imperfect, corrupt and even harmful.

He starts by explaining how as a child and young man his affections and interests were first drawn one way and then another. He was distracted and unfocused and had no clear idea of what constituted a valid and good relationship. It wasn't until he became a Cistercian that he found a way of

---

[41] Aelred: Spiritual Friendship, 61.
[42] Ibid., 47.

understanding friendship in a more settled and mature way—where friendship became a source of support and not a distraction, where its foundation was the pursuit of God rather than material or secular enjoyments.

Aelred was taking a risk writing about spiritual friendship as personal friendships in monastic communities were generally frowned upon. Benedict's Rule does not say anything explicitly about friendship but does condemn "murmuring" and the formation of factions.[43] But, the development of particular friendships will have been a concern to abbots in case they led to a sexual relationship—a serious deviation from the monastic rule and a danger to the soul (not just because homosexuality was viewed as sinful but because chastity was prized so highly). It is exceedingly important to understand that Aelred is not talking about the type of love and friendship one would form or experience in normal everyday life. His writings were for other monks and must be read and understood in that context.

I suspect that what Aelred was doing was acknowledging the very basic part of us all that attracts us to some people and repels us from others. He had seen it in himself and in those around him. He knew that bonds between monks, even if they rarely had the opportunity to speak to each other, did arise and his own experience was that these friendships could help rather than hinder on the path *but* one had to choose these friends wisely.

Aelred saw friendship as a natural state for human beings—not a state that should be avoided but one that should be encouraged in a wise fashion.[44] He wrote that "scarcely any happiness whatever can exist among mankind

---

[43] Aelred: Spiritual Friendship: Roby, introduction, 16.
[44] Aelred: Spiritual Friendship, 69.

without friendship"[45] and "the best medicine in life is a friend".[46] Aware of the pitfalls of certain types of friendship he set out to show how monks could choose spiritual friends.

Aelred also uses *Spiritual Friendship* as a vehicle for answering critics about him having "favourites" and also to forward the case that friendship between monks is perfectly acceptable if it is based in true spiritual love. He had found this to be true in his own life and had seen the damaging effects in abbeys where the abbots were so severe that no friendships were allowed to flourish at all.

Aelred was writing this after a lifetime of experience and it is often only with hindsight that we learn that not everyone can be a good friend, that we do not always choose wisely, that some friendships cause great pain and harm, and that true friendship is a very precious gift. To try impart this in a way that can be understood and worked with by others is not an easy task and I think Aelred fails but only because it is pretty much an impossible task. No matter how much he outlines the qualities to look for and those to avoid, the spiritual foundations and the role of God, human nature is such that it will always find a way to excuse some failing in another if there is attraction or interest. It is just the way we are, and some of us learn by experience and some do not.

The wisdom needed to ascertain a true friend in the way Aelred outlines is not something than can be taught and that is why no matter how much Aelred tries to explain how to chose a spiritual friend he fails in the sense that not everyone will be able to follow his example. His words may be used as inspiration or guidance but the experience that they speak

---

45 Ibid., 71.
46 Ibid., 72.

from is unique to Aelred and is not an experience that would have been shared by all the members of his community.

The other aspect of the book that is problematic is Aelred's use of examples from his own life—of friends and how much he loved them and how they helped him. These are included to show and explain to his readers what he means by spiritual friendship but that is not how they have been seen. During his own lifetime these, by some, were seen as further proof of him having "favourites" and not as he intended. Whilst Aelred was not an idealist in the sense of believing that all friendships were good, he was an idealist in believing that spiritual friendship was a friendship that could be achieved by all his monks. Theoretically it was, but realistically it wasn't and his words could have been used to justify friendships that were far from spiritual.

I understand that, more recently, Aelred's writings on friendship have been interpreted, by some, as indicating homosexual tendencies. In my opinion, this is a further example of how *Spiritual Friendship* has been misunderstood. Aelred really was going out on a limb acknowledging the basic need of humans to communicate and to form close bonds even within monasteries. He knew from his own experience that true spiritual friendship with others was possible and he assumed that others could arrive at the same experience and understanding. Perhaps one of Aelred's failings was that he genuinely believed that everyone could achieve the degree of spirituality and union with God that he had and, sadly, that was not and is not the case. Perhaps Aelred did know this but felt that his words would be of great benefit to some and that the risks of misunderstanding were worth the potential benefits.

# On The Soul

In his last years, Aelred devoted some of his time to writing *On the Soul*. Like all of his writings, *On the Soul* reflects the depth and certainty of Aelred's beliefs and faith but his writing is not dogmatic. The book is divided into three parts and is written as a dialogue between Aelred, as abbot, and a monk named John. The subject matter is the "soul". Aelred's style is instructive and informative rather than lecturing and the dialogue format, once again, makes it easier for the reader to follow.

Aelred argues that the soul is in the body but that it is not in a specific location—rather it resides throughout the body, everywhere at the same time. The soul is not a body nor is it made up of any combination of earth, fire, air or water, and we are unable to observe it directly with our conventional senses. Aelred says that the soul is a form of "rational life" and different from the type of life found in trees, plants and animals. It is changeable and immortal in its own way but not in the way that God is. God is always the same and in the same state but this is not the case with the soul which is "drawn here and there by diverse wishes" and has the ability to be happy or sad.[47]

The key aspects of the soul are memory, reason and will, functioning together in a form of co-dependency.[48] Aelred relies quite heavily on the teachings and theories of St Augustine quoting him directly: "The soul, as anyone can easily see, gives life by its presence to this earthly and mortal flesh; it holds all its parts together and keeps them one and does not allow it to dissolve or waste away."[49] Having

---

[47] Aelred: On the Soul, 40.
[48] Ibid., 52.
[49] Ibid., 57.

outlined what the soul is and what it is not, Aelred moves on to debate what the soul can accomplish with or without the senses through memory, reason and will.

In the third part, he explores what happens at the time of death and discusses how we are able to communicate with saints, angels, and God. The change in style of this section has led to speculation that *On the Soul* was never completed or that it is indicative of Aelred's failing health. I much prefer Marjory Lange's interpretation of the difference as being Aelred preparing his monks for the time of his own death which he knew was not far away.[50] It is a comforting section focusing on how prayer still links the living with dead.

*On the Soul* is, however, possibly the least satisfying of Aelred's book as it poses questions such as "what is the origin of the soul?" but provides no answers. As Squire puts it, Aelred "seems to get lost in his own puzzles and questions".[51] Walter Daniel claimed that the third part of the book was unfinished[52] but the discussion does appear to have reached a natural conclusion.[53] It is possible that the book, at Aelred's death, was still a work in progress, a sort of first draft, in which Aelred posed the questions that, as yet, no one had answered and which he intended to work on, through contemplation, and maybe furnish some answers. The fact that he was unable to provide answers at the time simply puts him on par with other writers in the twelfth century and today.

---

[50] Lange, 401–420.
[51] Squire, A., 131.
[52] Daniel, W. 42.
[53] Squire, A, 130.

# Chapter 8

# The Final Years

The last ten years of Aelred's life were exceedingly busy ones. He was securing the future of Rievaulx, involved in state and religious affairs, writing, travelling and, struggling with health issues.

As we move into these final years, we have a clear picture of the type of person Aelred was. Gilbert of Hoyland, abbot of Swineshead, saw him as a man "of serene and modest spirit, equable and unworried, alert in mind, deliberate in speech". He had often watched him in conversation and remembered how "patiently he suffered interruption."[1] Gilbert had been present at some of the spiritual discussions held in Aelred's quarters and witnessed firsthand how Aelred interacted with his monks. Aelred's style may have been informal yet his spiritual authority was greater than that of many abbots who enforced a more rigid system on their monks.

Gilbert also wrote that Aelred was quick "to listen, slow to speak, but not slow to anger. How is he to be described as slow to anger? I would rather say he was not in the race!"[2] Jocelin of Furness, in his Life of Waldef, viewed Aelred as "a

---

[1] Daniel: Powicke, introduction, xxxiii.
[2] Aelred: Mirror of Charity; Dumont, intro., quoting Gilbert of Hoyland, 48.

man of the highest integrity, of great practical wisdom, witty and eloquent, a pleasant companion, generous and discreet. And, with all these qualities, he exceeded all his fellow prelates of the Church in his patience and tenderness. He was full of sympathy for the infirmities, both physical and moral, of others."[3]

Aelred was not universally liked and had his critics but he handled them with patience, understanding, and compassion. A man like Aelred "who offers no sharp angles to the outsider and has more to forgive than to be forgiven, provokes unreasoning exasperation in envious or unbalanced minds".[4] He was a man "whose love was great enough to prove that greatness does not need to be brutal, and that to be a saint one does not have to despise human affections."[5]

Aelred was "one of the busiest and most sagacious men of his time".[6] He acted as "father, pastor, physician, judge, brother to all the differing types of men who crowded into his monastery".[7] He was "a capable manager and administrator… he understood the process of land accumulation by the abbey and the importance of lay benefactors in this".[8] "His was a pure and steady candle-flame; not a blaze that could light up a dark sky or consume a forest. Yet he had a personality unique among the writers and abbots of that age. Highly gifted, strong both to do and to suffer, he was an abbot whose wisdom appeared primarily in his personal love and sympathy, and his wise direction of souls."[9]

---

[3] Daniel: Powicke, introduction, xxxiii.
[4] Ibid., lxv.
[5] Aelred: Spiritual Friendship; Roby introduction, 14.
[6] Daniel: Powicke, introduction, xvi.
[7] De Waal, 116.
[8] Jamroziak, 217.
[9] Aelred: Pastoral Prayer; Knowles, introduction, xi.

# Health

Aelred had health problems throughout his life. The illnesses he suffered from were thought to be osteoarthritis, kidney, and urinary stones.[10] He was also hypersensitive to touch which indicates a form of fibromyalgia:

> "I have seen him suspended in mid-air in a linen sheet, held by a man at each of its four corners being carried to relieve himself or from one bed to another. A mere touch affected him like a piercing wound, and his cries revealed the measure of his pain".[11]

Given the amount of travel Aelred still conducted in the last ten years, it does seem that his health problems were, to some extent, cyclical rather than constantly present. It is only four years before his death that Walter Daniel describes him as still riding a horse and undertaking long journeys to Scotland.[12] In March 1163 he was one of the witnesses at Westminster to Henry II's confirmation of an agreement between Robert II, bishop of Lincoln and Robert, abbot of St Albans, about Episcopal rights.[13]

Reading the descriptions of his suffering and the fact that the episodes were cyclical rather than constant I suspect his problems were related to his diet. Fibromyalgia, extreme joint pain, and kidney stones have been identified in some individuals as being caused by a build up of naturally occurring food chemicals such as Salicylate. Salicylate is found in fruit, vegetables, herbs and spices, and is a chemical

---

10 Fergusson P. & Harrison, 128.
11 Daniel, 39.
12 Ibid., 46.
13 Daniel: Powicke, introduction, xciii.

that some people are unable to process easily. When there is a build up within the body physical problems manifest themselves but then, as the body clears the excess, the symptoms abate and so the cycle begins again.[14] Aelred's vegetarian diet will have been exceedingly high in Salicylate and possibly other food chemicals such as solanine.[15]

Regardless of the cause, his physical problems had to be lived with and accommodated. The General Chapter of 1156 allowed Aelred certain dispensations to enable him to carry on with his role as abbot. He was allowed to eat and sleep in the infirmary and was no longer restricted to doing things at certain times but was given the freedom to choose when he could best do things. Aelred was not fully easy with these changes and rejected many offered comforts even to the extent of fasting and refusing herbal treatments.

His biggest concession was to have rooms built for him alongside the infirmary from where he could conduct abbey business as usual, ensuring he was always available to his monks and to benefactors. Whilst Walter Daniel describes Aelred's room in the infirmary as a "cell" and "small" the reality was a little different. There was probably more than one room and the rooms were big enough to accommodate a group of people, at least two beds, some basic furniture and a small chapel where he kept his book of psalms, Confessions of St Augustine, St John's Gospel, relics of saints and a little cross that had once belonged to Henry Murdac.[16]

---

[14] Race, 109, 143-54.
[15] Ibid., 157-8.
[16] Squire, 129.

## The Last Few Years

During the last four years Aelred ate and drank very little: "by his unbelievable fasting he lost altogether, and no wonder, the desire for food". He refused anything that might alleviate his symptoms and grew very thin: "The excessive emaciation of his body and the thinness of his face gave an angelic expression to his countenance."[17]

It is tempting to suggest that Aelred's health problems prevented his involvement in issues outside of Rievaulx but, as we have seen, he was still travelling widely. It is probably only in the very last year that Aelred slowed down but of that we cannot be totally sure. Walter Daniel tells us that during Aelred's last year "a dry cough racked his breast and, added to all his other various infirmities, so weakened and wearied him that sometimes, when he came back to his cell after mass in the church, he could for an hour neither speak nor move but lay as though unconscious on his pallet".[18]

# The Rievaulx Family

Rievaulx continued to expand and Aelred worked tirelessly to ensure the abbey had benefactors, the resources that it needed and protection. In 1164, he was involved in the establishment of an agreement between Cîteaux and Sempringham, the Cistercians and the Gilbertines, on various issues of land and personnel. He was also involved with issues within Rievaulx's daughter houses.

---

[17] Daniel, 49.
[18] Ibid., 54.

## Melrose

Aelred visited Melrose in the early summer of 1159 and was present when a deputation came from St Andrews to offer Waldef the post of bishop. Although Aelred urged him to accept, Waldef refused on the grounds that he knew his end was near. On 3 August Waldef died and was buried in the chapter house at Melrose.[19] The new abbot, William a monk from Melrose, was elected as abbot on 27 November 1159 and was blessed two days later in the abbey church by the bishop of Glasgow.[20]

The year 1164 saw the foundation of Melrose's fourth daughter house at Coupar Angus in Perthshire. Abbot William was also faced with other issues at the time as news of miracles occurring around Waldef's tomb began to spread and the abbey found itself having to deal with pilgrims. In an attempt to protect the privacy of the abbey William attempted to play down the miracles but, unfortunately for him, this alienated him from his monks and he had to resign.[21] His resignation did not take place until 1170, three years after Aelred's death, so some form of compromise must have functioned for a number of years—a compromise no doubt suggested by Aelred. In the spring of 1166, a recorded visit to Melrose tells us that Aelred was still able to travel.[22]

## Dundrennan

Very little information has survived regarding the early years of Dundrennan Abbey. We know that Aelred was in contact with Fergus, Lord of Galloway, the founder of Dundrennan

---

[19] Fawcett and Oram, 23.
[20] Ibid., 23.
[21] Ibid., 23.
[22] Daniel: Powicke, introduction, xciv.

and known to Aelred from his days at the Scottish court.[23] In 1159 Aelred is recorded as helping settle a dispute between Fergus and his sons. Family disputes aside, the relationship between Galloway and Scotland was deteriorating and the 1160s saw Malcolm, the Scottish King, taking action against Galloway that led to Fergus giving up his lands and spending his last years in a monastery.[24]

Two years before his death, Aelred visited Dundrennan and stayed there for about a week. Walter Daniel specifically mentions the visit as he cites it as an occasion of an Aelred miracle. Walter says that Aelred "was lodged in a poor leaky hovel, as the conventional buildings were not finished".[25] Apparently the buildings were still of a temporary nature and made of wood. The monks made a bed for Aelred in the corner of a room but were dismayed at how wet the whole hut became when it rained: as Walter puts it, "no part of the roof, not even a space of a couple of feet, was free from the penetration of the rain".[26] It rained virtually the whole time they were there and everybody was soaked except for Aelred who was never wet by even a single drop. As soon as Aelred's bedding was moved from the corner the rain found its way in and that area was as wet as any other in the hut. Walter Espec's former chaplain, William, was at that time Dundrennan's sacristan and is cited as one of the witnesses to the event.[27]

There are problems with this incident as described by Walter. Dundrennan abbey had been existence for at least twenty years and the Cistercians required that basic

---

[23] Daniel, 45.
[24] Brooke, D., 92–5.
[25] Daniel: Powicke, introduction, lxx.
[26] Daniel, 74.
[27] Ibid., 75.

buildings were constructed before any monks arrived. There was sufficient land granted by Fergus for the abbey's development,[28] so there was no reason why stone buildings had not all ready been constructed. Even if they hadn't been there is absolutely no reason for any wood building not to have been made as watertight as was possible in the twelfth century.

There is architectural evidence to suggest that Dundrennan flourished in the twelfth century and that the main parts of the abbey were under construction between 1150 and 1175.[29] In the 1160s Dundrennan was expanding and having to draw up agreements with Holm Cultram abbey about land use rights.[30] It is also the case that Aelred was an influential abbot and the abbot of Dundrennan would not have allowed Aelred to be housed in such poor conditions. Brooke puts it very well when she writes: "Any abbot in his right mind would have given up his own bed and slept on the floor rather than let such a thing happen!"[31]

Perhaps it is the case that Walter's account of Galloway and the people within it was coloured by the fact that Fergus had been defeated. There was nothing to gain by being pleasant about him or his people. As a defeated group they were an easy and convenient target for blame. Even Aelred in his *Battle of Standard* is quite vivid in his description of their barbarity. The Galloway people were seen as being different, and worse they had been defeated.[32] Fergus had been in support of the election of William Fitz Herbert as archbishop of York and so his stance was contrary to the position of the

[28] Brooke, D. 90.
[29] Robinson, 105–106.
[30] Oram, 2000, 252.
[31] Brooke, D., 89.
[32] Ibid., 99.

Cistercians who supported Henry Murdac. Oram writes that: "It was left to the Cistercians to exact a particularly malicious revenge: the libelling of the reputation of both Fergus and his people".[33]

Whilst this might explain some of what Walter writes it doesn't explain his description of the poor housing conditions at Dundrennan. It could very well be the case that he is right and building work was delayed at Dundrennan but if that was the case then surely monks would not have moved in. However, if the account is simply inaccurate, why did Sylvanus, Aelred's successor as Rievaulx's abbot and Dundrennan's abbot at the time of the visit, not spot the error? It is, sadly, a mystery that cannot be resolved in this book.

It is recorded that Aelred celebrated the feast of St Cuthbert in a small Kirkcudbright church. This is noted as being the 20 March and most likely to have taken place during the above visit to Dundrennan.[34] These snippets of information about Aelred's activities are tantalising as they clearly set Aelred apart from other abbots who travelled from their mother house to their destination, remained for the allotted time, and returned. Aelred it seems was not one for being enclosed only with his fellow monks. He was, at least to some extent, a man of the people.

# The Wider World

The Cistercians continued to expand and gain power. By 1160 it is calculated that there had been fifty Cistercian bishops, ten Cistercian cardinals and a Cistercian pope.[35]

---

[33] Oram, 2000, 67.
[34] Daniel: Powicke, introduction, xciv.
[35] Fergusson & Harrison, 4.

Aelred was the most influential Cistercian abbot in England and his power was exercised politically as well as spiritually. For England, it was a time of relative peace and economic stability after the anarchy of Stephen's reign but in the wider domain of the church's influence he was witnessing the end of a period of papal stability.

## Papal Crisis

In 1159, Alexander III was elected as Pope. It was, however, not a straightforward affair as a small, but powerful, group of cardinals elected an anti-pope, Victor IV. Various political manoeuvrings led to the anti-pope gaining support in some countries. The Cistercians were horrified at this attempt to undermine the true Pope and many Cistercian abbots, including Aelred, joined in pleading Alexander's case with their Kings.

Aelred, along with Arnulf, bishop of Lisieux, is credited with persuading Henry II to support Alexander.[36] The campaign was successful and Alexander became Pope but his reign was fraught with problems; and the next twenty years saw four more anti-popes. The clear direction and inspiration that Aelred must have experienced under Pope Eugenius was over. Aelred, like many of the Cistercians of his time, had been caught up in a movement of reform with high ideals. They changed their lives and believed their example would bring about permanent changes to the wider church. These ideals were now shaken.

Aelred was older and wiser and having always been a man of balance he will have been saddened by these changes but will have maintained a sense of perspective. He will have turned his mind and heart to the work that he could do—

---

[36] Daniel: Powicke, introduction, xlviii.

ensuring Rievaulx's future and helping others with their vocation.

## Watton Nun

At some point around 1159, the "Watton Nun" incident took place. A record of the events has been handed down to us as Aelred's own account has survived.[37] Watton, in East Yorkshire, was a Gilbertine double house accommodating nuns and cannons strictly segregated from each other. The story is cruel and a reflection of the repression and harshness that could take place.

The nun had been accepted into Watton at the age of four and had never settled into the way of life. (Problems frequently occurred when vocations were not freely entered into which is why the Cistercians would only accept adults.) The nun, whose name we do not know, was having an affair with a Gilbertine brother. When discovered by her fellow nuns, she was beaten and incarcerated in solitary confinement, her legs in chains. Within a short time it was discovered that she was pregnant. Gilbert was notified of the situation and ordered that the brother responsible be found and handed over to the nuns. This was done and the disgraced nun was forced to cut off her lover's testicles. The man was returned to the brothers and we hear nothing else about him.

The nun's story, however, continues. Miraculously, one day she was found no longer be pregnant with no sign of a child or evidence that a birth had taken place. One of the fetters of her chains had also fallen off. She had apparently dreamt that an angel had come to her and removed the baby. Gilbert, the head of the order, asked Aelred to investigate the

---

[37] Aelred: Watton Nun.

incident. Aelred travelled to Watton to hear the story directly and to visit the nun. Whilst unhappy at the violence that had been perpetrated, he praised the nuns' desire to pursue chastity and punish wrongdoing. On visiting the nun, he declared that the fetter had not been removed by the nun or others but by God and should, therefore, not be restored. A short while later he was informed that the second fetter had also fallen away. He saw these events as a sign of how sinners can be forgiven.

Regardless of how we may view such an event, we cannot dispute that, at the time, the miraculous nature of the event was accepted by all the participants. By turning the ending of the incident into a miraculous one, the attention was diverted from the "sin" and the Gilbertines' reputation was saved. The fact that neither Gilbert nor Aelred actually saw the nun when she was pregnant does make me wonder whether a switch had taken place and that the "miracle" was a way of the nuns saving face but, I guess, we will never know. We also do not know for whom or why the story was written down by Aelred. It could have been that he was asked to do this by Gilbert as a way of having a record of the incident that was by an objective outsider.

## Life of Edward

Prompted by reports of miracles taking place at Edward the Confessor's shrine in Westminster Abbey, moves were made, in 1138, to obtain formal papal canonisation. Various delays ensued and nothing happened until, in 1160, Henry II successfully took up Edward's case.

In 1163, Pope Alexander agreed to the canonisation, probably in return for Henry's recognition of him as the true Pope. On 3 October, Edward's relics were solemnly translated to a new shrine in Westminster abbey. This was a national event attended by all with power and influence. The prelate who presided over the translation was the newly appointed archbishop of Canterbury, Thomas Becket.[38]

Aelred attended the ceremony and preached a sermon to the congregation. He had been asked by Abbot Laurence of Westminster to write a new biography of Edward which was completed in time for this event.[39] It is a work that is very closely based on the "Life of Edward the Confessor" written by Osbert de Clare when an attempt was made to have Edward canonised in 1138. The prologue continues the theme of Aelred's *Genealogy of the Kings* by extolling the sanctity of English Kings. Aelred assures the new king that Edward had prophesied on his deathbed that it would be he, Henry, who would be the cornerstone uniting, in himself, the English and Norman heritages and hence the country.

## Thomas Becket

In 1162, Henry II ensured that Thomas Becket was elected as archbishop of Canterbury. Once Becket was recognised in his new role by the Pope, he embraced it with vigour and resigned from his post as chancellor. Becket's status changed from one of dependency on the King to one of being his own master and the harmony that had existed between the two men soon evaporated. As chancellor, Becket had aggressively pursued royal rights and now applied the same tactics and energy to championing the cause of Canterbury and the church. He was soon in open conflict with Henry and their relationship deteriorated.

---

[38] Daniel: Powicke, introduction, xlix.
[39] Aelred: Edward the Confessor.

It would have been interesting to have Aelred's assessment of Thomas Becket as it seems inevitable that they met but sadly no record remains. Powicke speculates that Aelred's sympathies most likely lay with the king rather than Becket: "Peace was restored in England, why disturb it".[40] We know that Becket wrote to Rievaulx asking for their prayers and received a reply that was probably from Aelred.[41] The letter is quite general and tells us little about Aelred's actual views or feelings. "The writer urges the archbishop to protect the Church against the election to bishoprics of unsuitable youths. He hopes to be able to discuss this and other matters with the archbishop privately."[42]

By October 1163, Henry had reached breaking point with Becket and stripped him of all the secular honours he had acquired as chancellor. This, of course, did not bring an end to the conflict. They came further into dispute over the issue of secular courts punishing ecclesiastics for offences already dealt with by church courts and on the freedom to appeal to Rome. To the dismay of many of his followers, in 1164, Becket accepted many changes that were then incorporated by the King in the Constitution of Clarendon. Becket then changed his mind and attempted to reject them. A bitter struggle followed.

Becket was accused of fraud whilst chancellor and sent for trial. On the day of his trial in Northampton, Becket denied the jurisdiction of the royal court claiming the issue was one of ecclesiastical independence and appealed to Rome. That night, believing he was in danger, Becket resolved on flight. He escaped on horseback from the north

---

[40] Daniel: Powicke, introduction, xlix.
[41] Burton, 293.
[42] Daniel: Powicke, introduction, 1–1i.

gate of the town. A Gilbertine brother who was with him guided him through a night of torrential rain along unfrequented roads to Lincoln. At Lincoln he stayed with a friend of the Gilbertines and disguised himself by putting on the tunic and shoes of a lay brother and assumed the name "Christian".

At dusk on the second day they travelled by boat down the river Witham until they reached Hoyland-in-the-fens, a lonely hermitage belonging to Sempringham and forty miles away from Lincoln. He stayed there for three days and then travelled the ten miles to Boston to continue his journey by water to Haverholme, another Gilbertine house. He then made his way south, stopping at Chicksand priory (Gilbertine) and continued travelling by night and hiding by day until he, and his companion, reached the Kent coast and sailed from Eastry to Oye near Gravelines on 2 November.[43] Becket did not to return to England during Aelred's lifetime.

Unfortunately for Rievaulx, Becket took refuge in the Cistercian abbey at Pontigny in France, between 1164 and 1166. Henry II threatened to confiscate all Cistercian land in England whilst the Cistercians gave refuge to Becket. During this time, some of Rievaulx's benefactors, including the patron, attempted to take land back from the abbey. Fortunately, the pope's intervention with threats of excommunication prevented losses to Rievaulx but it must have been a seriously worrying time for Aelred as Rievaulx's abbot.[44]

---

[43] Graham, 16–18.
[44] Harvey, 72-3.

## Gilbertines in Crisis

Aelred's relationship with the Gilbertine order was an ongoing one and, in 1164, he was at Kirkstead in Lincolnshire to sign an agreement between the Cistercians and Gilbertines regarding ownership of granges and land. He will have been dismayed at the attempt to discredit Gilbert which took place around this time.

At some point in the mid 1160s, the lay brothers of Sempringham, led by Ogger and Gerard, revolted against Gilbert. The focus of their concerns was alleged moral lapses resulting from the nearness of nuns and cannons. No resolution was forthcoming and the issue was set before Pope Alexander. Gilbert received tremendous support— Henry II and various bishops wrote to the pope stressing the inaccuracy of the lay brothers claims and praising Gilbert.

The support for Gilbert is surprising as the revolt arose around the time of the Gilbertines involvement in Thomas Becket's escape from England. In early 1165, Henry II had summoned Gilbert and his priors to Westminster to answer a charge of having sent money abroad to Becket. This placed the order in great danger as the penalty was exile. Henry was not present but at the last minute sent notice that he would deal with the case himself. On hearing this, Gilbert, who had refused to deny the charges, confessed his innocence. He had up until that point refused to do so—on the grounds that if he had been asked for money by Becket, and had it available, he would have believed the right course of action would have been to help his fellow member of the church.

Henry was an astute political leader. The Gilbertine order was the only truly British order, Gilbert was nearly eighty and respected by many, and Henry did not want any excuse for papal intervention in English affairs. All the charges against Gilbert were dropped.

## Albigensians

The Albigensians, also known as the Cathars, began to send missionaries to Western Europe in the 1140s.[45] In 1165, some thirty Cathars from Germany, men and women, came to England. They were unsuccessful in spreading their message and were condemned in a provincial council, held at Oxford in 1166, punished and exiled.[46]

Aelred makes specific reference to the Cathars as heretics condemning marriage, ridiculing the sacrament of the altar, denying the resurrection of the body and preaching the uselessness of baptism.[47] It is quite obvious that Aelred had no real understanding of what the Cathars stood for when he says that the reason they condemn marriage is because they want to have "in common all the women who belong to their sect".[48] In fact, the leaders of the Cathars, known as perfects, abhorred sexual intercourse, were vegetarian and went in for severe fasting.[49] Ironically enough the austerity of their life went a long way to mirroring that of a Cistercian monk.

# Rule of Life for a Recluse

Somewhere around 1160-62, Aelred wrote *Rule of Life for a Recluse* at the request of his sister who had adopted the life of a religious recluse.[50] We, sadly, do not even know his sister's name. Neither do we know where she lived her life as

---

[45] Lynch, 222.
[46] Poole, 230.
[47] Aelred: On the Soul, 65–67.
[48] Ibid., 65–67.
[49] Lynch, 223.
[50] Aelred: Rule of Life for a Recluse

a recluse. I suspect that the location was most likely in the North of England as I am convinced from reading the work that Aelred saw her on many occasions. Squire also speculates that the location may have been in the area between Hexham and Durham.[51]

Within the *Rule of Life for a Recluse*, Aelred provides specific instructions on how recluses should behave and interact, or not, with other people. He provides a structure for how each day should be spent and how prayers and activities should be adapted to the church's year. He tells us that there are two elements in the love of God: "Interior Dispositions" and the "Performance of Works". The "Performance of Works" arise from aspects of the life such as fasting, vigils, work, reading, prayer and poverty.

The "Interior Dispositions" are developed through prayer and meditation. To assist in this process, he outlines a threefold meditation focusing on the past, present and future.[52] The past involves meditation and reflection on the life of Jesus. The present involves examining present day experiences and seeing how they reflect the love of God which includes giving thanks for having a healthy body, for being born near to other people of faith, and for God's forgiveness and love. The future is death and marks the end of the present and the start of the future; the meditation focus is the judgement that will take place and the options of heaven and hell.

Aelred tells us that the work is as a result of repeated requests from his sister and is intended as a guide not solely for her but also for women in a similar position. We must assume that, by the time Aelred wrote this work, his sister

---

[51] Squire, 119.
[52] Aelred: Rule of Life for a Recluse, 79-102.

had already been living by a set of rules. It, also, seems likely that Aelred will have visited his sister at various times over the years and that the Rule is the result of their conversations together. His sister's request for the rule may have been a more literal type of request—one to set the Rule down on paper so that it could be shared with others rather than one specifically for herself.

Given the type of person Aelred was, it is unlikely that he would have delayed in producing a Rule for his sister if she had been in need of one. It is my view that the Rule was written towards the end of Aelred's life because it was a work that evolved over time and, I believe, in discussion with his sister. By writing the Rule down it could be shared with, and passed to others and it was: the first part of the Rule "is one of the earliest English instructions for recluses, and as such was used by many who came after".[53]

By introducing the Rule as being for his sister, Aelred once again uses the devise of familiarity. By addressing the work directly to an individual the work becomes more accessible to the reader. It also provides a reason for the existence of the work so that writer is exonerated from being solely responsible for, at least, the idea. The other reason that leads me to believe the Rule is a work of collaboration is that it is different to so many of Aelred's other writings. The worldly experience, from the perspective of a woman, and the fewer biblical references, at least in the first part, all indicate an evolving discussion over the years and not solely an intellectual exercise. Aelred himself writes, in respect of contact with men:

> "You my sister, have never needed, thank God, to
> be reminded of these things," and, in respect of

---

[53] Aelred: Rule of Life for a Recluse; Knowles, introduction, xii.

quantity and quality of food, "it is surely unnecessary to impose any rule upon you, my sister. From your very childhood until now, when age is taking its toll of your body, you have scarcely taken enough food to keep yourself alive. I shall try however to formulate a rule for others and you can decide whether it will be helpful to them".[54]

# Cures, Miracles, and Prophecy

Miracles and cures, whilst not commonplace, were an accepted part of life in the twelfth century, so the recording of these types of events in respect of Aelred is in no way unusual, in fact it would have been strange if no such accounts existed. When Bernard of Clairvaux travelled in the Rhineland preaching the Crusade a close record of his miracles was kept and added to by his fellow travellers.[55] In respect of Aelred, Walter Daniel outlines a number of these incidents whilst Aelred was at Revesby and then during his Rievaulx abbacy. The instances outlined below all come from the latter era.

One of the monks had a particularly bad stomach disease that was known to lead to sudden death. The illness had become so severe that the man lost the ability to speak. Aelred was away from Rievaulx at the time but, on his return, placed his forefinger on the monk's mouth and said "speak, my brother, in the name of the Lord". The monk found himself replying to his abbot, the stomach pains reduced and his health was restored. [56]

---

[54] Aelred: Rule of Life for a Recluse, 52, 59.
[55] Bredero, 26.
[56] Daniel, 43.

Argar, one of the abbey's shepherds had been dumb for three days and was brought to Rievaulx. Aelred touched his lips with something, Walter says he does not know what it was, and said "speak, I command you in Christ" and the shepherd's power of speech was returned.[57]

A young monk with heart problems had become so ill he was in the last stages of dying. Aelred rushed to his own cell, "gathered together the relics of saints and the text of John's gospel", bound these to the sick man's chest and said "beloved son, may the Son of God make thee whole" and the monk "was relieved of all his trouble".[58]

On one occasion, Aelred and his companions were riding home to Rievaulx after a visit to Dundrennan abbey. Whilst still in Scotland they met a young man "with a frightfully swollen belly". The man was seriously ill after having, inadvertently swallowed a small frog, and asked Aelred to heal him. Aelred replied that it was not something he could do but that God could. He dismounted from his horse, inserted two fingers down the man's throat and prayed. The young man vomited, releasing the frog unharmed.[59]

When the Savignac order was incorporated into the Cistercians assistance was given to the abbeys to help them make the transition to the new way of doing things. Aelred sent a group from Rievaulx to Swineshead that included the monk once deemed to be "unstable". Whilst they were away, Aelred had a dream in which he saw that the unstable monk would die within a few days of his return to Rievaulx. Within five or six days of their return "he fell sick and was

---

[57] Ibid., 43, 68.
[58] Ibid., 44.
[59] Ibid., 47–48.

struck down by a most serious illness" and a few days later died.[60]

Walter Daniel further attributes the gift of prophecy to Aelred during the last few years of his life when he recounts how Aelred "ordered certain of the brethren to confess their sins before they had confessed and told them of things which they had done in secret, with details of time and place".[61]

# Final Days

Walter Daniel tells us that, a few days before his death, Aelred described himself to his monks as follows:

> "I have lived with a good conscience among you, for as I lie here, as you see, at the point of death, my soul calls God to witness that, since I received this habit of religion, the malice, detraction or quarrel of no man has ever kindled any feeling in me against him which has been strong enough to last the day in the domicile of my heart. I have always loved peace and the salvation of the brethren and inward quiet. By the grace of Christ I have commanded my spirit that no disturbance to the patience of mind should survive the setting of the sun."[62]

Although physically weak and in pain, Aelred's mind remained lucid until his death: "Until the end his five senses were unimpaired, but the words which he spoke were brief and broken".[63]

---

[60] Ibid., 35–36.
[61] Ibid., 51.
[62] Ibid., 57–58
[63] Ibid., 59.

By Christmas Eve 1166, Aelred knew he was approaching his death but he was still able to address the monks in Chapter and attend other services that day. On Christmas day, he preached a sermon during Chapter:

> "He was present at Mass also at Vespers when he sat by the steps of the presbytery. After Vespers he was received into his cell and laid upon his bed by the hands of his servants. For two hours he lay as though unconscious and half dead". [64]

Walter visited him a while later and commiserated with him about the pain he was experiencing, Aelred replied: "Yes, my son, yes, yes, just as you say; I am greatly vexed by the agonies of this sickness; by the will of the Lord Jesus there will soon be an end to all this trouble." Some of the monks needed to discuss abbey business with him but Aelred was too tired.[65]

Over the next few days, Aelred grew weaker and on 3 January he ordered all the monks to be summoned to him. Walter records Aelred's words to them:

> "Often I have begged your permission when I had to cross the sea, or it was my duty to hasten to some distant region, or I had occasion to seek the King's court; and now by your leave and with the help of your prayers I go hence, from exile to the fatherland, from darkness to light, from this evil world to God..."[66]

Aelred then advised them how to choose his successor and encouraged the younger monks to listen to the advice of the

---

[64] Ibid., 56.
[65] Ibid., 56.
[66] Ibid., 57.

older monks and the priors. He ended his address with a blessing and an expression of good wishes for all the monks.

The next day Roger, the abbot of Byland, anointed Aelred with holy oil in preparation for his death. Walter describes being with Aelred during those last days as "an awe-inspiring experience" and was convinced that angels were conversing with his abbot.[67] Members of the Rievaulx community remained with Aelred throughout the day and night. On the day before he died, Richard the abbot of Fountains and Roger abbot of Byland with nearly all the monks and some of the conversi were with him. Scripture was read to him and, whilst he could no longer speak, he would at times smile or move his hands in recognition of Jesus' humility or the disciples' faithfulness. Walter sat with him that day and held his head in his hands.[68]

On 12 January 1167, Aelred was placed "as the monastic custom is, on a hair-cloth strewn with ashes, and as the brethren with the four abbots who were there gathered about him, he surrendered his spotless spirit into the hands of his Father, and was at rest in Christ".[69] His body was washed and anointed and the funeral took place the next day. He was buried in the chapter house next to Abbot William.

In later years his remains were moved to the church and were still there in the sixteenth century before the dissolution of the abbey: John Leland reports seeing Aelred's shrine glittering with gold and silver.[70] Aelred came to be venerated as a saint and his official feast day is 12 January.

---

[67] Ibid., 59.
[68] Ibid., 61.
[69] Ibid., 62.
[70] Squire, 2.

"Our father is dead; he has vanished from our world like the morning sunshine, and many hearts long that this great light should flood with its brightness the memory of generations to come, and indeed of those still living for whom it shone in all its splendour."[71]

---

[71] Daniel, 1.

# End Word

It has been a pleasure to explore what Aelred's life may have been like back in the twelfth century. I have come to admire and respect him greatly and, through his religious writings, I have come to know a man who practised what he preached. I am convinced that he attained a level of spiritual understanding that alludes most of us whether in monasteries or outside of them.

Whilst I was brought up as a Catholic, my adult inclinations have always leaned towards Buddhism so I approached Aelred's writings with quite a large degree of trepidation and fully expected them to be either incomprehensible to me or very dogmatic. I was pleasantly surprised. It does take a little time to adjust to the style of language and the constant biblical references but, when you do, Aelred's message is beautiful and his style of teaching is delightful. There is humour, self-denigration, inspiration, humility and an overriding compassion for all. He exudes an inner peace and stillness that is comforting and healing.

Whilst writing this book I felt that Aelred's biggest flaw was that he believed that everyone could attain the same level of spiritual understanding as he had. As I complete this book, I am beginning to understand that actually this was

Aelred's greatest strength. He knew, and understood, that outwardly we may all be different but that inwardly we are all the same: each of us created in the image of God and, because of this, capable of reuniting our souls with their true nature. Did Aelred understand that not everyone would be able to do this? Yes, I think he did but he never compromised on knowing that it was in fact possible for each and everyone of his monks and lay brothers. He knew how fortunate they were to have been able to remove themselves from society and to have the time and support of others to pursue the Cistercian path. He kept Rievaulx's doors and his own heart open to all.

It seems that Aelred's writings were rarely used within the Cistercian order after his death until a revival of interest in the twentieth century. I don't find this strange as it will have been a rare abbot who didn't find Aelred's writings threatening in some way. It has always been easier for an abbot to maintain his distance from his monks rather than follow Aelred's example of making himself always available to his monks and viewing them as his equals. Aelred's style of abbacy was not one that could be easily emulated as it was only possible because of the type of person that he was.

I have enjoyed my journey with Aelred immensely and I hope you have enjoyed it too—thank you for sharing it with me. I, also, would like to extend my thanks to all the individuals who have, over the years, written about Aelred and translated his words—this book would have been impossible without you. I also send my thanks, back in time, to Walter Daniel without his work we would know very little about Aelred.

Sharla Race

# Bibliography

## Aelred's Writings

Various translations and editions of Aelred's writings have appeared over the years. The details below refer to the ones I have used during the writing of this book.

### Battle of the Standard

"The Battle of the Standard" in *Aelred of Rievaulx: The Historical Works*. Translated by Jane Patricia Freeland. Edited with an introduction by Marsh L Dutton. Cistercian Publications, 2005, 245–270.

### Genealogy of the Kings

"The Genealogy of the Kings of the English" in *Aelred of Rievaulx: The Historical Works*. Translated by Jane Patricia Freeland. Edited with an introduction by Marsh L Dutton. Cistercian Publications, 2005, 39–122.

### Hexham Saints

"The Saints of the Church of Hexham and their Miracles" in *Aelred of Rievaulx. The Lives of the Northern Saints.*

Translated by Freeland, J.P., edited with an introduction by Dutton, M. L. Cistercian Publications, 2006, 65–108.

## Lament for David

"Lament for David, King of the Scots" in *Aelred of Rievaulx: The Historical Works*. Translated by Jane Patricia Freeland. Edited with an introduction by Marsh L Dutton. Cistercian Publications, 2005, 45–70.

## Life of Edward

"The Life of Saint Edward, King and Confessor" in *Aelred of Rievaulx: The Historical Works*. Translated by Jane Patricia Freeland. Edited with an introduction by Marsh L Dutton. Cistercian Publications, 2005, 123–244.

## Life of Ninian

"The Life of Ninian, Apostle of the Southern Picts" in *Aelred of Rievaulx. The Lives of the Northern Saints*. Translated by Freeland, J.P., edited with an introduction by Dutton, M. L. Cistercian Publications, 2006, 35–64.
Also, "The Life of St. Ninian" in *Two Celtic Saints: The Life of St Ninian by Ailred, and The Life of St Kentigern* by Joceline. Facsimile reprint by Llanerch Enterprises, 1989.

## Liturgical Sermons

*Aelred of Rievaulx: The Liturgical Sermons*. The First Clairvaux Collection: Advent-All Saints. Translated by Theodore Berkeley and M. Basil Pennington. Introduction by Basil Pennington. Cistercian Publications, 2001.

## Mirror of Charity

*Mirror of Charity*, Aelred of Rievaulx. Translated by Elizabeth Connor, introduction and notes by Charles Dumont. Cistercian Publications, 1990.

## On Jesus at the Age of Twelve

"On Jesus at the Age of Twelve" in *Aelred of Rievaulx: Treatises & Pastoral Prayer*. Introduction by David Knowles. Cistercian Publications, 1995.

## On the Soul

*Dialogue on the Soul*, Aelred of Rievaulx. Translated with an introduction by C. H. Talbot. Cistercian Publications, 1981.

## Pastoral Prayer

"The Pastoral Prayer" in *Aelred of Rievaulx: Treatises & Pastoral Prayer*. Introduction by David Knowles. Cistercian Publications, 1995.

## Rule of Life for a Recluse

"Rule of Life for a Recluse" in *Aelred of Rievaulx: Treatises & Pastoral Prayer*. Introduction by David Knowles. Cistercian Publications, 1995.

## Spiritual Friendship

*Spiritual Friendship*, Aelred of Rievaulx. Translated by Mary Eugenia Laker. Introduction by Douglass Roby. Cistercian Publications, 1977.

## Watton Nun

"A Certain Wonderful Miracle" in *Aelred of Rievaulx. The Lives of the Northern Saints*. Translated by Freeland, J.P., edited with an introduction by Dutton, M. L. Cistercian Publications, 2006, 109–122.

# Main Bibliography

Aird, W. M. *St Cuthbert and the Normans: The Church of Durham, 1071–1153.* Boydell Press, 1998.

Armstrong, K. *Holy War: The Crusades and their impact on today's world.* Papermac, 1992.

Baldwin, J. *Edinburgh, Lothians and Borders.* Stationery Office, 1997.

Barrow, G. W. S. *The Anglo-Norman Era in Scottish History.* Oxford University Press, 1980.

———— Kingship and Unity: Scotland 1000–1306. Edward Arnold, 1981.

Bartlett, R. *England under the Norman and Angevin Kings: 1075–1225.* Oxford University Press, 2000.

Benedict. *The Rule of Saint Benedict.* Translated by Abbot Parry, introduction and commentary by Esther de Waal. Gracewing, 2003.

Bernard of Clairvaux. *In Praise of the New Knighthood.* Translated by M. Conrad Greenia, Introduction by Malcolm Barber. Cistercian Publications, 2000.

———— *Life of St Malachy of Armagh.* Translated by H. J. Lawlor. SPCK, 1920.

Bible. NRSV Catholic Edition. Darton, Longman and Todd, 2005.

Bolton, B. M. 'The Cistercians and the Aftermath of the Second Crusade' in *The Second Crusade and the Cistercians.* Edited by Gervers, M., St. Martins Press, 1992, 131–140.

Bradbury, J. 'The Early Years of the Reign of Stephen, 1135-9' in: Williams, D. *England in the Twelfth Century.* Boydell Press, 1990.

Bredero, A. H. *Bernard of Clairvaux: Between Cult and History.* T & T Clark, 1996.

Brooke, C. *The Twelfth Century Renaissance.* Thames & Hudson, 1969.

Brooke, D. *Wild men and Holy Places: St Ninian, Whithorn and the Medieval Realm of Galloway.* Canongate Books, 1998.

Bulst-Thiele, M. L. 'The Influence of St Bernard of Clairvaux on the Formation of the Order of the Knights Templar' in *The Second Crusade and the Cistercians.* Edited by Gervers, M., St. Martins Press, 1992, 57–65.

Burton, J. *The Monastic Order in Yorkshire: 1069–1215.* Cambridge University Press, 2006.

Bynum, C. W. *Jesus as Mother: Studies in the Spirituality of the High Middle Ages.* University of California Press, 1982.

Christie, A. H. *The Abbey of Dundrennan.* Thomas Fraser, 1914.

Coppack, G. *The White Monks*: The Cistercians in Britain 1128–1540. Tempus, 2000.

Dalton, P. *Conquest, Anarchy & Lordship: Yorkshire, 1066–1154.* Cambridge University Press, 1994.

Daniel, Walter. *The Life of Ailred of Rievaulx.* Translation and introduction by Maurice Powicke. Oxford University Press, 1978.

De Waal, E. *The Way of Simplicity: The Cistercian Tradition.* Darton, Longman and Todd, 2005.

Dickinson, J. C. *The Later Middle Ages: From the Norman Conquest to the Eve of the Reformation.* Adam & Charles Black, 1979.

Dumont, C. Personalism in Community according to Aelred of Rievaulx. *Cistercian Studies, Vol XII, 1977:4, 250–271.*

Dutton, M. L. 'The Conversion and Vocation of Aelred of Rievaulx: A Historical Hypothesis' in: Williams, D. *England in the Twelfth Century.* Boydell Press, 1990.

Farrar, W. Early *Yorkshire Charters, Vol. I.* Ballantyne and Co., 1914.

——— *Early Yorkshire Charters, Vol. II.* Ballantyne and Co., 1915.

——— *Early Yorkshire Charters, Vol. III.* Ballantyne and Co., 1916.

Fawcett, R. and Oram, R. *Melrose Abbey.* Tempus Publishing, 2004.

Fergusson P. & Harrison S. *Rievaulx Abbey: Community, Architecture, Memory.* Yale University Press, 2000.

Gervers, M. 'Donations to the Hospitallers in England in the Wake of the Second Crusade' in *The Second Crusade and the Cistercians,* Edited by Gervers, M., St. Martins Press, 1992, 155–161.

Graham, R. *St Gilbert of Sempringham and the Gilbertines: A History of the only English Monastic Order.* Elliot Stock, 1903.

Harrison, S. *Byland Abbey.* English Heritage, 1992.

Harvey, T. E. *Saint Aelred of Rievaulx.* Allenson, 1932.

Hindle, B. P. *Roads, Tracks and their Interpretation.* Batsford, 1993.

——— *Medieval Roads and Tracks.* Shire Publications, 2009.

Horton, M. C. *The Story of Cleveland.* Cleveland County Libraries, 1979.

Hutchinson, W. *A View of Northumberland with an Excursion to the Abbey of Mailross in Scotland, Vol II.* Charnley & Whitfield, 1776.

Inglis, H. R. G. Ancient Border Highways: The Minchmoor (Catrail) Road, the Wheel Causeway, the Annandale Forest Road, the Well Path, and the Enterkin. *PSAS, Vol. 58 (1923-24), 203–23.*

Jamroziak, E. *Rievaulx Abbey and its Social Context, 1130–1300: Memory, Locality and Networks. Brepolis, 2005.*

Knowles, D. *The Monastic Order in England: 943-1216.* Cambridge University Press, 1950.

Lange, M. E. A Reading of Aelred of Rievaulx's De Anima: Trough Ciceronian Dialogue to Personal Testament. *Cistercian Studies Quarterly, Vol. 45, 2010:4, 401-420.*

Lawrence, C. H. *Medieval Monasticism: Forms of religious life in Western Europe in the Middle Ages.* Longman, 1992, 2<sup>nd</sup> edition.

Leclerq J. *Monks and Love in twelfth century France: Psycho-Historical Essays.* Oxford University Press, 1979.

Lees, B. A. *Records of the Templars in England in the Twelfth Century.* London, 1935.

Lynch, J. H. *The Medieval Church: A Brief History.* Longman, 1992.

Merton, T. St Aelred of Rievaulx and the Cistercians I. *Cistercian Studies, Vol. XX, 1985:3, 212–223.*

——— St Aelred of Rievaulx and the Cistercians II. *Cistercian Studies, Vol. XXI, 1986:1, 30–42.*

——— St Aelred of Rievaulx and the Cistercians III. *Cistercian Studies, Vol. XXXII, 1987:1, 55–75.*

——— St Aelred of Rievaulx and the Cistercians IV. *Cistercian Studies, Vol. XXIII, 1988:1, 45–62.*

——— St Aelred of Rievaulx and the Cistercians V. *Cistercian Studies, Vol. XXIV, 1989:1, 50–68.*

Moffat, A. *Kelsae: A History of Kelso from Earliest Times.* Mainstream Publishing, 1985.

Morton, J. *The History and Antiquities of the Abbeys of Jedburgh, Kelso, Melrose and Dryburgh.* W. H. Lizars, 1832.

Musgrove, F. *The North of England: A History from Roman Times to the Present.* Blackwell, 1990.

Nicholl, D. *Thurstan: Archbishop of York, 1114–40.* Stonegate Press, 1964.

Offler, H. S. (Ed). *Durham Episcopal Charters 1071–1152.* Northumberland Press, 1968.

Ohler, N. *The Medieval Traveller.* Boydell Press, 1995.

Oram, R. *The Lordship of Galloway.* John Donald, 2000.

—— *David: The King Who Made Scotland.* The History Press, 2008.

Orme, N. *From Childhood to Chivalry: The Education of the English Kings and Aristocracy, 1066–1530.* Methuen, 1984.

Page, W. *A History of the County of York: Volume 3.* Victoria County History, 1974

Partner, P. *The Murdered Magicians: The Templars and their Myth.* Oxford University Press, 1982.

Poole, A. L. *Domesday Book to Magna Carta: 1087–1216.* Oxford University Press, 1992, 2nd Edition.

Race, S. *Change Your Diet and Change Your Life: Food Intolerance & Food Allergy Handbook* Tigmor Press, 2001.

Raine, J. *Priory of Hexham, Vol. I.* Surtees Society, 1864.

Rice, F. *The Hermit of Finchale.* Pentland Press, 1994.

Robinson, D. (editor). *The Cistercian Abbeys of Britain: Far from the Concourse of Men.* Batsford 2002.

Runciman, S. *A History of the Crusades, Vol 2. The Kingdom of Jerusalem.* Penguin 1990.

Scammell, G. V. *Hugh du Puiset, Bishop of Durham.* Cambridge University Press, 1956.

Seward, D. *The Monks of War: The Military Religious Orders.* Eyre Methuen, 1972.

Simeon. *Simeon's History of the Church of Durham.* Translated by Joseph Stevenson. Facsimile Reprint 1993 by Llanerch Publishers.

Sommerfeldt, J. R. *Aelred of Rievaulx: Pursuing Perfect Happiness*. Newman Press, 2005.

Squire, A. *Aelred of Rievaulx: A Study*. SPCK, 1973

Stenton, D. M. *English Society in the Early Middle Ages*. Penguin, 1991.

Stenton, M. D. (editor). *Preparatory to Anglo-Saxon England: The Collected Papers of Frank Merry Stenton*. Oxford University Press, 2000.

Sykes, J. *Local Records Vol. 1: Northumberland, Durham, Newcastle upon Tyne and Berwick upon Tweed*. Patrick and Shotton, 1973.

Tatton-Brown, J and Crook, J. *The Abbeys and Priories of England*. New Holland, 2006.

Welch, M. *Anglo Saxon England*. B.T. Batsford, 1992.

Whitelock, D. Ed. *The Anglo Saxon Chronicle*. Eyre & Spottiswode, 1961.

Williams, D. *England in the Twelfth Century*. Boydell Press, 1990.

Williams, D. H. T*he Cistercians in the Early Middle Ages*. Gracewing , 1998.

Young , G. *A History of Whitby and Streoneshall Abbey Vol. 1*. (1817). Caedmon of Whitby reprints, 1976.

# Index